ISBN 978-1-333-87850-4
PIBN 10631251

1 MONTH OF
FREE
READING

at

www.ForgottenBooks.com

By purchasing this book you are eligible for one month membership to ForgottenBooks.com, giving you unlimited access to our entire collection of over 700,000 titles via our web site and mobile apps.

To claim your free month visit:

www.forgottenbooks.com/free631251

English
Français
Deutsche
Italiano
Español
Português

www.forgottenbooks.com

Mythology Photography **Fiction**
Fishing Christianity **Art** Cooking
Essays Buddhism Freemasonry
Medicine **Biology** Music **Ancient
Egypt** Evolution Carpentry Physics
Dance Geology **Mathematics** Fitness
Shakespeare **Folklore** Yoga Marketing
Confidence Immortality Biographies
Poetry **Psychology** Witchcraft
Electronics Chemistry History **Law**
Accounting **Philosophy** Anthropology
Alchemy Drama Quantum Mechanics
Atheism Sexual Health **Ancient History**
Entrepreneurship Languages Sport
Paleontology Needlework Islam
Metaphysics Investment Archaeology
Parenting Statistics Criminology
Motivational

A GUIDE FOR VISITORS

TO

KASHMIR

BY

JOHN COLLETT.

Enlarged, revised and corrected up to date

. BY

A. MITRA,

Chief Medical Officer, Kashmir,

WITH A ROUTE MAP OF KASHMIR.

———

CALCUTTA :

W. NEWMAN & CO., 4, DALHOUSIE SQUARE.

1898.

PREFACE.

———•———

THE increased facilities which have been provided during the last few years for visiting the beautiful Valley of Kashmir, and more particularly the opening of the Jhelum Valley Cart Road, is inducing a much larger number of persons than in former years to spend their short leave in a visit to the lovely scenery to be found in the Valley. This short Guide Book is intended to aid visitors by a description of the principal routes, and by giving other information that may prove useful to them. The map which accompanies the Guide shows the principal routes which are practicable to the casual visitor. The information has been brought down to the year 1897.

CONTENTS:

CONTENTS—*(concluded.)*

A GUIDE FOR VISITORS

TO

KASHMIR.

———✳———

INTRODUCTION.

THERE is, perhaps, no land under the sun which has received such praise in prose or rhyme as the valley of Kashmir. And, indeed, it is very beautiful— " an emerald of verdure enclosed in a radiant amphitheatre of virgin snow " The valley, which is peopled by a primitive type of the Aryan race, is intersected by a beautiful meandering river, and is covered with luxuriant fruit trees and fragrant flowers, with majestic chinars and silvery poplars. Behind all stand the majestic snow-clad mountains. Truly has the Persian poet said

> " Do not call it Kashmir, it is a rival
> Of the celestial fairy land.
> It is a Paradise on the face of the earth."

Vigne thus speaks of the scenery of Kashmir ·—
" Softness mantling over the sublime — snugness, generally elsewhere incompatible with extent—are the prevailing characteristics ; and verdure and the forest appear to have deserted the countries on the northward

in order to embellish the slopes from its snowy mountains, give additional richness to its plains, and combine with its delightful climate to render it not unworthy
of the rhyming epithets applied to it in the East—

Kashmir—Be nazir— without an equal.

Kashmir—Junat nazir—equal to Paradise."

Located in the midst of rocks and mountains,
Kashmir is a fertile alluvial valley, which yields
produce beyond the dreams of the cultivator in the
sun-scorched plains of India. "You have but to
tickle the land with a hoe and it laughs with a harvest."
Streams of pure water gush from the rocky sides of
high mountains to enrich the soil and assuage the
thirst of man and beast. The deep waters of the lake
reflect the summits of snow-capped mountains. In
spring, the valley is covered with a mass of flowers;
in autumn, the trees are painted with gorgeous tints ; and
in winter, a mantle of virgin snow lies over the land.
It was in this country that the ancient Aryans built
temples and monuments, the Buddhists reared their
majestic places of worship, and the great Moguls laid
out their pleasure gardens, and fountains, and grottos for
the almond-eyed beauties of the Imperial harem. The
ozone-laden mountain air and the temperate climate
form a delightful contrast to the heat of India and the
biting cold of Central Asia. Elphinstone says :—

" It is placed by its elevation above the reach of the
heat of Hindustan and sheltered by the surrounding
mountains from the blasts of the higher regions; it
enjoys a delicious climate, and exhibits in the midst of
snowy summits a scene of continual verdure, and
almost of perpetual spring."

To an invalid Kashmir is health-giving; to an archæologist it affords ample material for research; to an artist it presents Nature's loveliest and most sublime sceneries; to a geologist many abstruse and still undiscovered problems of strata and foliation; to a botanist a large field of still unclassified flora; to an ethnologist and philologist a puzzling inhabitant and language; and last, but not least, to the sportsman one of the best hunting grounds for large game in the whole world.

The number of visitors to the beautiful vale of Kashmir will certainly increase year by year, now that the valley is connected with the Punjab by a good cart-road, cut along the mountain side. The road has already given a great impetus to the trade of Kashmir, and ought to gradually develop all the resources of the valley.

It is supposed that the first European who penetrated into the valley of Kashmir was Xavier, a Jesuit, who visited it in the time of the great Akbar. In the year 1665, Bernier, a French physician, accompanied the Mogul Emperor Aurangzebe to the valley. The third European, another Jesuit, Father Desideri, passed a winter in Kashmir in 1714. George Forster travelled through Kashmir in 1783, when the valley was reft from the Crown of Delhi by the Afghans. Forty years after, when Kashmir was under the rule of Ranjit Singh, the Lion of the Punjab, it was visited by Moorcroft. In these days, when a traveller can drive from Rawalpindi to Baramulla through the valley of the Jhelum river in two days, it is not easy to realize that Moorcroft could not travel over this road for fear of his life.   Victor Jacquemont followed in 1831 by the permission of Ranjit Singh.   Next came Wolff, a missionary, in 1832.   Baron Hugel, Vigne, and Henderson met in Srinagar in 1835, and recorded their meeting on a black marble slab.   This interesting relic, however, has recently disappeared, probably stolen by some unromantic peasant to do duty for a curry-stone.   The inscription ran :—

Three Travellers :

Baron Carl Von Hugel, from Jamu,

John Henderson, from Ladak,

Godfrey Thomas Vigne, from Iskardo,

Who met in Srinagar on the 18th November, 1835, have caused the names of those European travellers who had previously visited the vale of Kashmir to be hereunder engraved :

Bernier	...	1663
Forster	...	1786
Moorcroft, Trebeck, and Guthrie	...	1823
Jacquemont		1831
Wolff	...	1832

The valley has now, however, as previously stated, been connected with the plains of India by a cart-road, and is annually visited by a large number of strangers from all parts of the world.   A Royal Prince, the Duke of Connaught, two Viceroys, Lords Ripon and Lansdowne, and two Commanders-in-Chief, Sir Donald Stewart and Lord Roberts, are among those who have been attracted to Kashmir.   Easier access with India and contact with foreign peoples and things are rapidly altering the primitive simplicity of the inhabitants and the Government, but the majestic mountains, the icy springs, the murmuring brooks, and the picturesque landscape will for ever retain their grandeur and beauty in spite of civilization and its influences. A day may come when the iron horse will penetrate into the valley; when Srinagar, the capital, will be a fashionable station with luxurious hotels and all the comforts of civilised life ; when steam power will revolutionize the industries and develop the resources of the country ; when in place of mat-covered boats, comfortable barges and house-boats will float upon its lakes and river. But the tourist in Kashmir will always turn his gaze from the works of man to the glorious beauties of Nature, and will look up with awe to the majestic Nunga Parbat and the hoary-headed Harmukh. The sylvan charm of Lolab, the flowery spring and the autumnal foliage of Lidar, the rivulets of Achhobat and Vernag, the Woolar with its reflections of snow-capped mountains, and the Jhelum winding its course through fertile fields and banks lined with the stately chinar, with the panorama of Pir Panjal as a background, can never lack admirers

Thomas Moore sings in his immortal " Lalla Rookh "

> " The vale of Kashmir,
> With its roses the brightest that earth ever gave,
> Its temples and grottos, and fountains as clear
> As the love-lighted eyes that hang over their wave "

Bernier, the French physician, who visited the valley in 1664 with Aurangzebe, has left a most interesting account of Kashmir. Archibald Constable publishes an English edition of his travels. Before Bernier, Xavier gave to the world his impressions of Kashmir in a work

entitled " Hajns de Rebus Japonicis, Indicis, etc."
(Antwerp, 1605). Forster's letters giving the nar-
rative of a journey from Bengal to St. Petersburg were
published in 1783. Other old books on travels in
Kashmir are—" Researches and Missionary Labours "
by the Rev. Jos. Wolff, " Correspondence of Victor
Jacquemont," Moorcroft's " Travel," Vigne's " Travels in Kashmir, etc.," and Baron Hugel's " Travels
in Kashmir and the Punjab."

Of later publications the following may be mentioned.
Knight's " Diary," Drew's " Kashmir and Jammu
Territories," Bellew's " Kashmir and Yarkand,"
Wakefield's " Happy Valley," Wilson's " The above
of snow," Colonel Torren's " Travels," Sir Richard
Temple's " Travels in Kashmir, Hyderabad, and Sik-
kim." " The Valley of Kashmir " by W. R. Lawrence,
C.S., C.I.E., is a complete gazetteer of Kashmir,
and gives valuable and authentic information about the
country and its people. Besides containing accurate
details regarding the Kashmiris, their habits and customs, religion and language, and occupation and industries, it gives information about the history, geology, botany, zoology, mineralogy and archæology of the
country. Kashmir possesses a history written by its own
historians known as " Raj Tarongini." It is now being
published by Dr. Stein, the gifted Principal of the
Lahore Oriental College, and has been partly translated by Fryer, Wilson, and Dutt. There are besides
many valuable works on Kashmir history in Sanskrit
and Persian, such as " Gulzari Kashmir " by Diwan
Kripa Ram, " Tarikha Kashmir " by Narayan Koul,
and " Tawarikh Kashmir " by Pandit Birbal Kachru

In the " Journal of the Asiatic Society of Bengal," Newel published a sketch of the Muhammadan history of Kashmir. Drew gives a full account of the geography of the countries around Kashmir, while on geology, Drew, Blanford, Lydeker, and Oldham are authorities. Lawrenee's information on the flora and fauna is accurate. Royle's " Himalayan Botany " may also be consulted by the botanical student, and Adam's " Wanderings óf a Naturalist in Kashmir," Ward's " Sportsman's guide,' and Kinloch's " Large Game Shooting in Tibet and the North-West " will be found useful by sportsmen. To the student of archæology, Cunningham's papers in the " Journal of the Royal Asiatic Society," and in the '' Archæological Survey Transactions," and Cole's 'Illustrations" will give valuable information. Elmslie's " Dictionary, " Wade's ''Grammar," Knowles' " Kashmir Proverbs and Kashmir Folk Stories " are useful books. Tourists are recommended Ince's " Kashmir Handbook," revised by Duke, Collet's " Guide for Visitors,'' first published in 1884, Neve's " Tourist's Guide to Kashmir, Ladakh, Skardu, etc.," and " Cashmere *en Famille.* "

CHAPTER I.

HINTS TO TRAVELLERS.

THE majority of visitors to Kashmir will naturally select the easiest route, which runs up the Jhelum valley. On arrival at Rawalpindi, the large military cantonment on the North-Western Railway, the traveller will find accommodation either in the dâk bungalow or in one of the many hotels. Here Messrs. Dhanjibhoy and Son, whose office is close to the dâk bungalow, should be communicated with. This company will furnish every information regarding the condition of the road, make arrangements about the journey, and furnish *tongas* and *ekkas*. Visitors will find dâk bungalows all along the road, but it often happens that tired arrivals find all the rooms fully occupied. Whenever, therefore, there is a rush, it is advisable for those who are travelling with their families to take tents. These moreover are indispensable when the valley is reached. Besides the usual baggage, several *kiltas*—long-barrelled baskets covered with leather—will be found useful for stores and cooking utensils. Sportsmen who have to carry their camps through jungles and over bad mountain paths will find *kiltas*, which are easily strapped on to the shoulders of coolies, leaving their arms free, absolutely necessary Tents and camp furniture can be hired at Srinagar. Travellers on their arrival in Kashmir have to make their own arrangements for cooking, etc. *Khansamahs* are to be found at

Srinagar, and can be temporarily engaged. But those travelling with their families would do better to bring with them a good *khansamah* and a sweeper. The latter class of servants are not easily available in Kashmir.

During the winter months *tongas* cannot run through to Kashmir, and in the early spring, when there is a good deal of rain, there are usually many slips on the Jhelum valley road, and the journey is not only likely to be interrupted, but is often dangerous. The Kashmir season, therefore, generally commences in the beginning of May and closes by the end of October. In Kashmir, the autumn is most lovely. On arrival in Kashmir the traveller, who has not brought his servants with him, will require a *khansamah* and a *bhistie*, who, besides supplying the camp with water, should assist in pitching tents and packing and unpacking the baggage; another servant will be wanted to assist the *khansamah*. All should be obliged to do any necessary work which falls outside the usual routine of their duties. If a boat is hired, the boatman is a very useful general servant. When ladies and children are of the party, an ayah and a sweeper will be wanted. The climate of Kashmir, though always bracing, is very variable. Waterproof coats, a mosquito curtain in summer, and waterproof coverings for the bedding are essentials. A suit of *puttoo*—a rough serge manufactured in the country—may be had at Srinagar for about Rs. 8, and though the style and fit would scarcely suit Bond Street, it makes a capital and comfortable wear for mountain travel. Visitors should not forget their dress suits, for Srinagar is not altogether uncivilised.

Every season there are a large number of Europeans at the capital.   On the Queen's Birthday a State
dinner is held, to which visitors are invited.   Military
officers attending are obliged to wear mess uniform.

On arrival at Srinagar, the Maharajah's Native Agent,
Babu Amar Nath Rai Sahib, is the first person to be
communicated with.   He speaks English fluently, and
is a very obliging and civil officer.   He will afford help
of every kind and give any information in his power.
He makes the arrangements for the hire of boatmen,
coolies, servants, etc., and settles all disputes that may
arise with regard to fares and the prices of purchases.
House accommodation is very limited in Kashmir ; many
of the old bungalows that were formerly available for
visitors are now occupied by the State officials.   There
are no dâk bungalows or hotels.   Travellers must, therefore, be prepared to live in boats or tents.   House-boats
are very comfortable to live in, but their number is
limited, and unless previous arrangements have been
made for the hire through an agent or a friend, it is
difficult to get one.   The rent varies between Rs. 30
and Rs. 50 a month.   Bachelors can only pitch their
tents in the Chinar Bagh, the other camping ground,
the Hari Singh Bagh, now being built over.   The
Chinar Bagh is, however, large enough to accommodate
all the visitors ever likely to require it.   The Munshi
Bagh is set apart for the tents of married visitors.   It
contains a row of *pucca* houses, but these are all occupied by permanent residents.   Further up the river is
Ram Munshi Bagh, an excellent camping ground.

The Resident lives in Srinagar during the summer
at the Residency—a fine house with a large garden by

the river side. It is customary to call on him and sign one's name in the Visitors' Book. A similar respect should also be shown to the Maharajah by entering one's name in the book kept for the purpose at the Palace Gate. The Maharajah and Resident leave Srinagar in the winter, but the Assistant Resident is at the capital when the Resident is away.

When out of Srinagar, the traveller should always take his servants with him. One of them should be allowed to have control over the others in all details; he will like to use the authority given him, and the others will obey him readily. The traveller will thus be relieved of a good deal of trouble. It is a good plan to make sure before every march that the proper number of coolies and ponies are present. The Kashmiris are willing workers, but they are ignorant of the ways of Europeans, and should be treated with patience and consideration. A traveller should avoid giving too much attention to details and little matters, and confine himself to stating his orders clearly and sticking to them. Attention to this will avert much unpleasantness and add materially to the enjoyment of a trip. On arriving at the end of a march, arrangements should be made with the *Tahsildar* or *Naib Tahsildar* at the nearest village for the hire of coolies and ponies for the next march. As long a notice as possible is needful, as the men and animals are often taken from the fields, sometimes some miles distant. For supplies during the journey, eggs, milk, butter, and fowls can always be had at a reasonable price. Those who penetrate out of the beaten tracks for shikar purposes, should provide themselves with all necessaries from Srinagar, where all kinds of European stores of excellent quality are obtainable. The traveller should personally pay the coolies at the end of each day's march, and a good supply of two anna, four anna, and eight anna pieces should be kept, so that each man can be paid separately. If a rupee is to be divided amongst three or four, there is frequently a quarrel. Indian coin is accepted eagerly everywhere in Kashmir. In Srinagar currency notes and cheques are easily negotiable. The Punjab Banking Corporation has a branch in Srinagar, where every kind of banking business is transacted. At Srinagar supplies are fairly good. Imported articles, such as kerosine oil and sugar, are expensive, but all indigenous articles are cheap. Pure milk can be obtained everywhere. The water-supply of Srinagar is now abundant and good. Fish can be had in abundance. It may be noted here that the roe of Kashmir fish should on no account be eaten, as the result is fearful gastric irritation. Bread can be had at Srinagar. A basket of excellent vegetable can be obtained from the Library garden for the modest sum of four annas.

For the return journey from Srinagar, *tongas* should be booked beforehand either at Dhanjibhoy's Srinagar office, or by telegraph to the Agent at Baramulla.

In the appendix will be found the rules, sanctioned by the Government of the Maharajah, for the guidance of European visitors, civil and military, and full information regarding the hire of coolies, ponies, etc.

CHAPTER II.

ROUTES.

THERE are several routes into the Happy Valley, but the easiest, and therefore the most frequented one is from Rawalpindi, *via* Murree. The traveller takes a *tonga* at Rawalpindi, and drives all the way to Srinagar. The cart-road is open to every kind of wheeled traffic, and throughout the route accommodation and supplies are available. Those who prefer a less frequented route should leave the railway at Gujrat, 71 miles from Lahore, and proceed by *tonga* to Bhimber, 28 miles from Gujrat, the border village of Kashmir territory, and at the foot of the lower range of mountains, and thence march the 167 miles to Srinagar over the Pir Panjal pass, which lies at an elevation of 11,500 feet above sea level The distance is covered in twelve marches, but the paths are difficult and require much climbing. This is the historical route which was used by the Mogul Emperors in their summer visits to the valley. In point of grandeur and magnificence, the scenery on the road cannot be surpassed. The other alternative route is *via* Jammu, and begins at the railway terminus Tawi, at the foot of Jammu hill, and crossing the Banhal pass (9,200 feet high), enters the valley at Vernag. This route is, however, reserved for His High-ness the Maharajah, and Europeans are not allowed to travel by it without special permission. The road is difficult, and supplies are not always available. The other

routes into the valley are (1) through Poonch to Baramulla, and (2) the Abbottabad route, which joins the
Jhelum valley road at Domel. The former road turns
off from Thanna Mundi, the sixth march on the Pir Panjal route, thus avoiding the ascent over the pass. The
route by Abbottabad joins the Jhelum valley road at
Domel. In the winter, when the snow lies heavy over
the Murree hills, this latter road is a convenient one.
There are several other less known routes, but they are
very seldom used. All the routes, except that up the
Jhelum valley, are difficult and full of obstructions,
such as boulders, masses of rock, and unbridged or
badly bridged streams. A few rest-houses are located
along the Jammu road, but they are in a very dilapidated condition. Supplies are obtainable only with the
very greatest difficulty.

JHELUM VALLEY ROAD.

The railway journey ends at Rawalpindi, the great
military station.

Station		Distance.	1st Class Ry. Fare.	Time.
			Rs. As. P.	
Calcutta to Rawalpindi	...	1,437 miles.	120 0 0	54 hours.
Delhi do.	...	483 ,.	32 10 0	22 ,,
Lahore do.	...	173 ,,	10 13 0	10
Bombay do.	...	1,412 ,,	88 4 0	67 ,,

At Rawalpindi may be found a dâk bungalow and several good hotels. All necessaries for a journey of several
months are obtainable here. On arrival, arrangements
must be made for a seat in the mail *tonga*, or for a
special *tonga* which carries three passengers besides a
fairly large quantity of personal baggage. *Ekkas* are

available for servants and heavy baggage. The mail *tonga* covers the journey to Baramulla in two days. It starts from Rawalpindi early in the morning, and arrives in the evening at Garhi, where it halts for the night ; and then starting at daybreak, reaches Baramulla at 3 P.M. In the summer, when the days are long, if there is no interruption on the road, a *tonga* will probably aecomplish the journey as follows :—

1st day.—

    Rawalpindi, leave at 5 A.M.

    Murree, reach at 10 A.M., breakfast at Sunnybank hotel, start at 11.A.M.

    Kohala, reach at 3-30 P.M.

    Domel, reach at 6-30 P.M., halt for the night.

2nd day.—

    Domel, leave at 5 A.M.

    Uri, reach at 10-30 A M.

    Baramulla, reach at 3-30 P.M.

The road between Rawalpindi and Srinagar is 195¼ miles long, and is divided into the following fourteen stages :—

Number.	Name.	Height above sea level.	Distance.	Remarks.
		Feet.	Miles.	
	Rawalpindi to -			
1	Barako ..	1,720	13½	Dâk Bungalow.
2	Tret ...	4,000	12	Ditto.
3	Murree (Sunnybank) ...	6,050	11¼	Hotels Murree. 7,507 feet above sea level and 38½ miles from Rawalpindi.

Number.	Name.	Height above sea level.	Distance.	Remarks
		Feet.	Miles.	
4	Kohala ...	2,000	27½	Dâk Bungalow, Telegraph Office.
5	Dulai ...	2,181	12	Dâk Bungalow.
6	Domel ...	2,319	9½	Dâk Bungalow, Post and Telegraph Office, Dispensary.
7	Garhi ...	2,750	13	Dâk Bungalow, Post and Telegraph Office.
8	Hattian ...	3,080	10	Rest-house, Post Office.
9	Chakoti ...	3,780	11	Dâk Bungalow, Post and Telegraph Office
10	Uri ...	4,425	13½	Dâk Bungalow Post and Telegraph Office.
11	Rampor ...	4,825	13	Dâk Bungalow, Post and Telegraph Office
12	Baramulla ...	5,150	16	Dâk Bungalow, Post and Telegraph Office, Dispensary
13	Pattan ...	5,300	16	
14	Srinagar ..	5,204	17	... .

On leaving Rawalpindi, the *tonga* drives over a good level road, lined with sheesham trees. At the 13th mile a hill stream is crossed, and half a mile further on is the Barako dâk bungalow. Shortly after leaving Barako the road enters low hills and gradually ascends, though the real climb does not begin till the 23rd mile is reached. On the right side of the road lies the Tret dâk bungalow. Beyond Tret the road rises rapidly to Murree and passes the Murree brewery at the 32½ mile. Above the brewery is the combined post and telegraph office of Goragalli. The *tonga* then runs up to the

Murree hills, and reaches the Commissariat godowns, where the road divides into two. The lower fork winds round the east face of the Murree hills and leads direct to Kohala and Kashmir. Sunnybank hotel is conveniently situated for travellers. From Murree to Kohala, 27½ miles, the road gradually descends. It is a long and somewhat tedious journey. On the opposite side of the valley are the territories of the Rajah of Poonch, the hill sides being dotted with the fertile fields of prosperous villagers. There is no dâk bunga-low between Murree and Kohala—a want which is often felt by travellers. Kohala is very hot in the summer. Crossing the bridge at Kohala, the traveller enters into the territory of the Maharajah of Kashmir. During the summer months the heat is intense on the road between Kohala and Chakoti, and it is advisable to travel across this in the early morning. A new bridge has recently been constructed, the old suspen-sion bridge having been swept away by the floods of 1893. The Jhelum valley road is a triumph of modern engineering. It is cut into the sides of the mountains and follows the course of the Jhelum as closely as possible The work was begun in 1880 and completed ten years after. The former road was barely more than a path, and was rough and steep, being in no wise practicable for wheeled traffic. After crossing the suspension bridge, the road passes Barsala and Chatar, and descends to the Agar Nadi. Below the 12th mile-stone from Kohala is the charming dâk bungalow of Dulai. Between Dulai and Domel, on the right bank of the river, a rapid mountain stream, known as the Nainsook, meets the Jhelum at the 16th

B

mile from Kohala.   Above the Nainsook both banks of
the   river   Jhelum   are   in   the   Maharajah's   territory.
Nine and a half miles from Dulai is Domel—the junction
of the " two waters ".—where the Kishnagunga runs
into the Jhelum   Here there used to be an excellent dâk
bungalow, extensive workshops, and a good bridge
over the Jhelum, but the great flood of 1893 swept
them all away.   Across the river, 1½ miles from Domel,
is the town of Muzaffarabad, which is the head-
quarters of the district of Muzaffarabad.   This district
includes all the hilly tracts between Baramulla and
Kohala.   Half a mile from Domel the Kishnagunga is
crossed by a bridge, which leads to the Abbottabad
road, *viâ* Garhi Habibullah

From Domel the road turns off at an acute angle
south-east and east.   The bungalow at Garhi is
charmingly situated.   From here it is possible to see
the *jhula* or rope-bridge over the Jhelum.   From
Garhi to Hattian the distance is 10 miles.   The scenery
is varied.   After passing the Garhi bungalow, some
plane trees (chinars) are to be met with, but these
are not so large and beautiful as those to be found
in the valley of Kashmir.   The climate of India
has now at last been parted with, and the more
bracing breezes from the beautiful mountains of
Kashmir refresh and invigorate the traveller.   There
is a rest-house at Hattian, but no *khansamah*.   Between
Hattian and Chakoti stands a noble chinar tree, near
which is a mountain stream of pure water.   Across
the river will be seen a mud fort, near which a Sikh
army was once totally annihilated by the Paharis.
From Chakoti to Uri the road rises considerably.   The

hill sides being formed of loose stones and earth, dangerous landslips frequently occur, blocking the road and interrupting traffic. The Jhelum flows at the bottom of the valley, noisy and turbulent, racing over big boulders and deep pools. The scenery is bold and purely mountainous. Here and there table-lands may be seen, on which are a few huts, hardly numerous enough to form a village One pities the lonely life of the inhabitants on these heights, almost entirely cut off from the rest of the world, many of the table-lands being on the opposite side of the river. Between Chakoti and Uri is Opi *nullah*, over which a new bridge is under construction. Not far from Chakoti are the ruins of a Muhammadan mosque of handsomely carved deodar. It is a fair specimen of the carving to be seen on many mosques in Kashmir. The building was probably erected on this spot in, commemoration of some famous *pir* or saint who died and was buried there. Such *ziarats* or burying places of saints are to be found all over Kashmir. Quiet, shady retreats, commanding lovely views, are to this day selected by many Muhammadans who aspire to be *pirs*. They live a life of solitary meditation, and are supported by the contributions of the faithful. They exercise a restraining influence upon the villagers, and some of them are treated with the greatest respect. In the distance is the fort of Uri, which was intended to command the road from Chakoti, and also one on the other side of Uri leading to Poonch. There is a capital little dâk bungalow at Uri. The jhelum runs very deep here, and a rope-bridge over it of strange construction will please the curious. It is used by the people who have patches of

cultivation on the small table-lands, on the lower range of
mountains, the approach to whose fields are often pre-
cipitous and always difficult.   These spots may be seen
on the left hand side of the road not far from Uri.   The
life of one person a year on an average is, say the people,
sacrificed in crossing the rope bridge.   To watch folk
crossing, the surprise is that anyone is able to get safely
across.   The bridge is merely a rope-ladder thrown
horizontally across the river, and one can well imagine
the difficulty and danger of stepping across the gaps.

Leaving the bungalow at Uri, the road makes a long
detour to reach the opposite side of the Namlah *nullah*.
On this part of the road there is a long and very lofty
range of mountains of slaty formation and nearly per-
pendicular sides.   Trees grow solitary or in clumps here
and there, and above and below there is a fine deodar
forest.   The bungalow at Rampor is prettily situated,
and commands a fine view of the lofty mountains opposite.   Leaving Rampor, the traveller passes a place called
Bunyar, where there is a workshop and a dispensary.
About a mile from Bunyar is an old temple, which must
at one time have been an imposing building, judging by
the great arched entrance and central court-yard.
Hindus make pilgrimages to this sacred spot from
Srinagar and even more distant places.   The road then
passes the village of Naoshera, from where there is a
rough and difficult path to Gulmarg   Passing Naoshera,
the road runs through a level plain called Kachema or
Little Kashmir, and then, following the course of the
Jhelum, reaches the valley of Kashmir at Baramulla.
Before the *tonga* road was made, the traveller had to
take a straight road over the pass of Baramulla, from

the top of which a beautiful view of the valley could be obtained.

Baramulla is a large town on the right bank of the river, which is crossed by a wooden bridge, similar to that at Srinagar and other places in the valley. There is a dâk bungalow at Baramulla, and boats are, as a rule, to be found waiting here for hire. The *tonga* road from Baramulla to Srinagar is now complete, but many travellers will prefer to change the jolting of the hill carriage for the more gentle and agreeable motion of a boat. The new road is nearly 33 miles long from the Agency road, Baramulla, to the Dudh-ganga bridge, Srinagar. The alignment is partly on the old foot-path, but for the most part it winds round the toes of the lower Kharewas, or takes a straight line across the many *jheels* which are met with on the line. Three and a half miles from Baramullà is the village of Kanaspura, and about a mile further on is the village of Dilna, where Dhanjibhoy & Co. have built stables on the left hand side of the road. Passing Sangrawan and Phutka, Choorah, eight miles from Baramulla, is reached. Here the Ningal river is spanned by three brick arches, and the two next bridges of importance cross the Choorah and Bulgam streams. After Bulgam (10 miles) the road takes a turn to the right through Rhinji, Tarpur, Khama-yar, and Phalalan, till Pattan is reached. This is the half-way stage between Baramulla and Srinagar, and here may be seen two excellent types of ancient Hindu temples in a very fair state of preservation. Passing the 16th mile at Pattan, the road takes a sharp turn to the left and crosses the Hanjvera *jheel* and bridge. About two miles further on is the village of Singhpura, and beyond that the bridge at Haratrat. The road now turns to the right again, and Meerghund, about 24 miles from Baramulla, is reached. Here there is a small rest-house. Sportsmen will find some excellent snipe and duck shooting on the extensive *jheel.* A couple of miles further on is Lawapura, from where the old road branches off to Gulmarg. The only other place of interest before Srinagar is reached is Chak, where the post horses are changed for the final stage. Passing Shalteng and Zankoot, where there is also some capital duck shooting, the Srinagar race course comes in view, 32 miles from Baramulla, and then Dudhganga bridge and poplar avenue leading to the new Amira Kadal. The rows of poplar trees are quite a feature of the road. The trees also serve the useful purpose of affording protection where the bank is steep and dangerous to *tongas* and carriages. The road was made by Mr. Allanson Winn, of Messrs. Spedding and Co.

The boats usually available at Baramulla are called *doongas.* They have bare floors, and the sides and roof are of matting. The stern is occupied by the boatman and his family. The smoke and strong odour from the kitchen is often unpleasant, and it is advisable to engage two *doongas,* one for the servants and kitchen and the other for the traveller's own use. As a rule no furniture is available, though some boatmen can provide a table and chair. Occasionally house-boats, sometimes furnished, can be arranged for.

The passage up the river is very beautiful ; the scenery a few miles from Baramulla is specially charming. The hills rise gradually almost from the

river banks; they are covered with verdure, and
undulate for long distances, rising and falling in
graceful irregularity.

The first day's progress up the river will probably
terminate at Sopur, where there is a rest-house, of the
barrack form, but in fair condition. About half-way
between Baramulla and Sopur is a village called Dubgao, situated at the junction of the river Pohra with the
Jhelum. There is a large quantity of timber here,
which is brought down the Pohra during the floods
in May and June and the rains in July and August;
after these months the water falls so low that navigation is impracticable. This timber is used in boat-
building and for other purposes. There is a very
beautiful grove of plane trees (chinars) here, there are
a greater number of these trees together than is usual,
and they are unusually large. A route to Lolah is up
the river Pohra. A few hours after leaving Dubgao,
Sopur is reached. Sopur is a corruption of Suryapur,
called after Surya, an engineer of old, who built many
dams, canals and villages in Kashmir. As the boat
slowly approaches the stream becomes wider, and near-
ing the town a Hindu temple is seen. Sopur is a place
much frequented by visitors to Kashmir, for it is close
to the Wular lake; there is capital mahseer fishing
there, and it is the starting point for the two marches
thence to Gulmarg; the distance is 17½ miles, and as
the road is good, the two marches may be easily taken
in one day. The view from the bridge at Sopur, looking down the river and towards the Wular lake, is very
pretty indeed. The Wular lake must be left to the
end of the summer season, before it can be visited in

the flat-bottomed Kashmir boats. Fuller notice of
this lake will be afterwards taken : at present it is
sufficient to mention that this lake, like all lakes
surrounded by mountains, is liable to the action of furious
hurricanes, which makes its surface like a small sea,
and renders crossing it very dangerous ; at the close of
the year these hurricanes rarely occur. Instead, therefore, of crossing the Wular lake, the boats are taken up
the Naru canal, which skirts the south side, and enters
the jhelum at Shadipore ; the time occupied is eight
hours, as the boat has to be punted in deep water the
whole way. The canal is partly filled with the *singara*
plant (Trapa Bispinosa), which produces a nutritious
nut in the autumn, when the boats go out and drag
up the nuts from the bottom, in from six to ten feet
of water. These plants may be seen covering an immense expanse of water.

At Shadipore is the junction of the river Sind with the
Jhelum. At this point there is a fine plane tree in the
stream, the roots of which are protected by a casing of
stone. Under this tree there is a *lingam*, an object of
worship to the Hindus. They have given the name
Shadipore, "the place of marriage," to the confluence
of the two rivers. Another version is that Shadipore
is a corruption of Sharadapur, called after the goddess
Sharada. Near Shadipore there is a bridge over the
Naru canal. The road over this bridge connects
Srinagar with Sumbal.

As the boat is slowly pulled along, after leaving
Shadipore, the traveller will notice that the river widens
greatly. Between Shadipore and Srinagar there are
only a few small villages called Sonar Boni (goldsmith's

chenars) and Shalteng, beyond which lies the Purana
Chowni or Kripa Ram's Chowni.

The approach to Srinagar is by no means imposing.
The wretched buildings, which the inhabitants occupy,
and which meet the eye before the city is entered,
indicate too faithfully the condition of the greater
number of houses in the Kashmir capital. The river
narrows as the first bridge is approached. The double
row of tall straight poplars half a mile long, seen close
by, has long been a feature of Srinagar. The effect of
this avenue is in nowise marred by the other rows of
the same trees in the immediate neighbourhood and along
the banks of the river. After passing under the first
of the seven bridges which cross the Jhelum within
Srinagar, the city is entered, and the shops of the
principal shawl merchants may be noticed on either
side, their names in English letters on the sign-boards
clearly indicating that English visitors are their best
customers. It will be necessary to more minutely
describe Srinagar afterwards ; at present the traveller
is looking for a spot whereon to pitch his tent for a
time, as already stated, house accommodation is very
limited. Visitors who have house-boats can moor
them above the first bridge or Amira Kadal, anywhere
between Lalmandi and Ram Munshi Bagh. The
Chinar Bagh, Munshi Bagh, and Ram Munshi Bagh
are suitable camping grounds. The Chinar Bagh is the
most favoured of the three. As the name indicates, it
contains many of these beautiful trees, but being on
rather low ground on the bank of the canal, which
connects the Dal lake with the jhelum, it is occasionally covered with water during the rains or floods.

Consequently the ground is nearly always damp, and a rise in the river may render a sudden departure imperative. The Munshi Bagh is set apart for married visitors, all bachelors being warned off. It is an excellent camping ground. Further up the river the Ram Munshi Bagh affords good ground for pitching tents.

JAMMU ROUTE.

The railway terminus for this route is Tawi, a station on the Wazirabad-Sialkote branch of the North-Western Railway. Beyond the river Tawi, which is crossed by a bridge, lies Jammu, built on a plateau. There is a State dâk bungalow here. From Jammu the stages are as follow :—

No.	Names of stages.	Height above sea level in feet.	Distance in miles.	Remarks
	Jammu to			
1	Nagrota ...	1,200	5½	
2	Dansal ...	1,840	12	
3	Udhampore ...	2,500	14	
4	Dhrumtal ...	4,800	15	
5	Batoti ...	7,500	13½	
6	Ramban ...	2,535	14	
7	Ramsu ...	4,070	14	
8	Deogal ...	5,580	12	
9	Vernag ...	...	10	Banhal pass 9,200 feet. State Telegraph Office
10	Islamabad ...	5,350	15	Post Office and State Telegraph Office.
11	Avantipore ...	...	16	
12	Srinagar ...	5,204	17	

The road is difficult and trouble may be experienced
in getting supplies, unless they have been previously
arranged for by order of the Darbar.   There is an
unfurnished rest-house at each stage, but no *khansamah.*
Travellers must take their own servants and carry camp
furniture.   The march from Jammu to Nagrota is short
and lies over boulders and long stretches of sand.
Between Nagrota and Dansal the road passes through
pretty scenery, partly along the side of a steep hill and
partly parallel to a stream with deep pools.   Udhampore
is a large town and the head-quarters of a district in
the province of Jammu.   From Udhampore to Dhrumtal
the road is nearly level, and the whole march lies along
the side of a deep gorge.   The view on the road is magnificent.   From Dhrumtal the road passes by Chinani.
The Hindus believe that their goddess Parvati was born
at this pretty village.   Passing Chinani, the Batoti pass,
7,500 feet high, has to be crossed.   A beautiful meadow
lies on the top, and a perfect view of the majestic
mountains around is obtained.   A new bridge spans
the Chenab river, the ruins of the old one being seen
near by.   The bungalow at Ramban is prettily situated.
The march from   Ramban to Ramsu is long and
tiring, over a wretched road.   At the 12th mile lies
Deogal, and then the Banhal pass, 9,200 feet high, has
to be negotiated.   From here to the valley of Kashmir
the road, recently constructed, is excellent.   About 1½
miles from the foot of the Banhal pass is the delightful
spring of Vernag.   It was here that the Emperor Jehangir wished to be carried in his dying hours.   The march
from Vernag to Islamabad is on a level road and calls
for no remark.

THE ABBOTTABAD ROUTE.

This route may be used when the snow lies heavy on the Murree hills and blocks the road. Abbottabad lies 42 miles from Hassan Abdul, a station on the North-Western Railway, 29 miles from Rawalpindi, and is reached in five hours by *tonga*. It is the head-quarters of the Hazara district, which comprises a part of the mountain valleys drained by the Doab and Hurroo rivers. The hill-sides are covered with timber. The town is named after Major James Abbott, first Deputy Commissioner of Hazara, from 1847 to 1853. From Abbottabad to Mansera the distance is 16 miles The road is good, but several deep *nullahs* have to be crossed. There is a good bungalow at Mansera. From here to Garhi Habibullah is 17½ miles. There is a shorter but more difficult path from Mangli *nullah*, on the eighth mile from Mansera, to Garhi Habibullah, where there is a rest-house. An *ekka* can travel as far as this. From Garhi Habibullah to Muzaffarabad is 12 miles over a rough and steep road. A difficult path leads to the top of a pass, 3,000 feet high, and then by a sharp descent the Maharajah's territory is reached. The Kishnagunga river is crossed by a bridge near Domel, and after the Jhelum has been passed the journey will be continued along the Jhelum valley road.

When the Afghans held Kashmir, the road from Kabul to the valley lay through the Khyber pass, and then *viâ* Peshawar and Hassan Abdul to Muzaffarabad, whence it ran along the right bank of the Jhelum through Katar to Baramulla. The traveller can see this old road from his *tonga* on the left bank of the Jhelum. Baron Hugel travelled out in the Kashmir by it, and there are engineers who are inclined to think that the Jhelum valley cart-road should have followed the same bank of the river. Landslips are too frequent on the other side.

The stages of the entire route from Hassan Abdul to Muzaffarabad, and thence along the right bank of the Jhelum, are as follows:—

No.	Names of stages.	Distance in miles.	Remarks.
	Hassan Abdul to—		
1	Haripur ...	20	By *tonga* to Abbottabad in five hours
2	Abbottabad	22	Dâk Bungalow.
3	Mansera ...	16	Dâk Bungalow Pay as two marches.
4	Garhi Habibullah	17½	Rest-house Pay as 1½ marches.
5	Muzaffarabad	12	Joins Jhelum valley road at Domel.
6	Hattian	17	No Bungalow, and supplies not available. Road very bad.
7	Handa	11	
8	Katar	12	
9	Shahdera .	12	
10	Gingh ...	14	
11	Baramulla ..	18	

THE PIR PANJAL ROUTE.

To Srinagar by Gujrat and Bhimber over the Pir Panjal Pass.

The route to the vale of Kashmir over the .Pir Panjal is often preferred to that *viâ* Murree by those who
do not mind roughing it a bit, on account of the really
magnificent scenery to be met with on the road. Formerly, before the Jhelum valley road was opened, it was
the custom to enter Kashmir by the Murree and leave
it by the Pir Panjal route. The whole of the way
during the descent from the top of the pass, 11,400 feet
high, such views and in such glorious variety meet
the eye that each march is a continual delight. The
scenery varies from the most extensive and marvellous
views of long and lofty ranges of mountains, their
tops covered with snow late into the summer, and
encircling the entire valley, down to the soft and
lovely landscapes that spread out beneath the traveller's
foot as he slowly descends into the far-famed valley of
Kashmir.

The route over the Pir Panjal is closed from about
the end of October till the beginning of May; but
even during this time there is an alternative route
from Thanna Mundi, the fifth march to Poonch. This
road is a long one, for it joins the Murree route to Uri,
two marches from Baramulla. Ladies sometimes, if
the pass over the Pir Panjal is covered with snow in
the early part of the season, take the Poonch route.

The railway from Lahore takes the traveller to
Gujrat. The dâk bungalow is about five minutes' walk
from the station. Gujrat is the head-quarters of the
district, and contains a population of about 18,000.
It has long been famous for its inlaid work in gold and

iron, known as Gujrat ware. About two miles from the town is the battle-field of the second Sikh war, at which was decided the fate of the campaign, ending in the annexation of the Punjab. The cemetery, which contains the remains of the officers who fell in this battle, is close to the mosque. It is surrounded by a high wall, but admittance can be obtained by applying to the guard in charge. There are no other local monuments of this decisive engagement. Some memorials of the occupation of Gujrat by the Mogul Emperors still exist ; and a famous Muhammadan saint in the reign of Shah Jehan, named Pir Shah Doulab, adorned the city with ·several buildings from the offerings of his visitors.

The journey from Gujrat to Bhimber is 28½ miles, and may be performed on a hill cart, though a traveller may engage a *tonga* to carry him two-thirds of the distance—up to Kotli, where there is a dâk bungalow. An *ekka* will cover the distance between Gujrat and Bhimber in about ten hours, although the last few miles are very trying, on account of the bad state of the road. Arrangements should be made the day before. There are two stoppages on the road to change horses. The last stage is very difficult, as the dry beds of some mountain streams have to be crossed, and the wretched " tattoo " often sticks in the deep sand and is unable to go any further. On reaching Bhimber without mishap, the traveller will find a rest-house, the first in the Maharajah's territories, which are entered at Bhimber. The Pir Panjal range can be seen all the way from Gujrat, and at Bhimber the foot of the hills is reached.

The following is a list of the marches and distances from Bhimber to Srinagar :—

No.	Names of halting places.	Distance in miles.	Remarks.
1	Bhimber to Saidabad	15	There is a rest-house at the end of each march, except at Ramoo; supplies do not include meat, but a sheep may sometimes be bought during a march. The Pir Panjal pass, 11,400 feet, is crossed on the march from Poshiani to Aliabad Serai
2	Naoshera ...	12½	
3	Changas Serai ...	14	
4	Rajaori	14	
5	Thanna Mundi ...	14	
6	Baramgalli ...	10½	
7	Poshiani ...	8	
8	Aliabad Serai ...	8½	
9	Hirpura	11	
10	Shupyan	8	
11	Ramoo	11	
12	Srinagar ...	17	
	Total ...	150½	

Taking the route over the Pir Panjal pass, the first march is from—

Bhimber to Saidabad, 15 miles.—The Aditak range is crossed near Sumani. The ascent is very steep and the road full of boulders. The river Bhimber has first to be crossed about six times, either on horse back or on the back of a cooly. In the rains this operation is not without danger, as the river runs down very rapidly. There is a nice spring of pure water near the staging bungalow at Saidabad, but drinkable water is not easily procurable during the march. The road is the worst in the whole journey. The Aditak range is the first of the three to be crossed before the Pir Panjal is reached. The ascent commences soon after leaving Bhimber, and the top of the range is reached by a rough, stony path. The view of the valley lying between this and the next

range is very pretty. Saidabad is seen below, surrounded by cultivated fields. The rest-house is similar to
those to be met with throughout the Maharajah's
territories. The situation is hot even early in
May. Here may be seen the ruins of the first of the
old Mogul serais on this route. They will be met with
at nearly every march, for the Emperors from Delhi
used this route. The modern rest-house has been built
in the same locality as the serais. The ruins at Saidabad
cover a good deal of ground. They are in the shape of
a quadrangle surrounded by a high wall. At one end is
a raised stone platform, on which was placed a throne
for the Emperor, who 'received there the obeisances of
the people and transacted public business. The remains of a small bazar, for the sale of supplies, and a
little mosque, where the Emperor and his retinue paid
their devotions during their stay, are also to be found
here. On a hill about 500 feet high,' a quarter of a
mile up the valley, in a commanding position, is a fort
built by one of the family of Runjit Singh. It is now
occupied by the State police.

If the nights are moonlight, the first two or
three marches from Bhimber should be made from
midnight to sunrise. The heat of the day is thus
avoided.

Saidabad to Naoshera, 12½ *miles.*—In this march the
second of the lower ranges is crossed. The road lies
along a valley for the first half of the way, and then the
ascent is short but rugged, and the descent long and
winding and very rough, over great blocks of sandstone.
During this march the great heat of the plains is passed,
and in the early morning the song of the cuckoo and

other birds may be heard. The scenery is pretty, the
sides of the hills are covered with trees, and the valleys
are luxuriant with vegetation of all sorts. There is a
Mogul serai here, and a Sikh fort. The rest-house is
like that at Saidabad ; supplies are limited to eggs and
chickens. The water at Naoshera is dirty, and comes
from an old well. There is no spring near the staging
bungalow.

Naoshera to Changas Serai, 12 ½ *miles.*—The distance on
all the marches seems to be rather arbitrarily fixed ; to
the traveller the time occupied is the best measure of the
distance. This march is long, hot, and tedious, but the
scenery is lovely. The road winds through the valley
of the river Tawi, and it must be followed, as there are
no bridges over the river. Before reaching Changas
Serai a wide plain is crossed, and then the river Tawi.
The rest-house may be seen on the high bank of the
river on the opposite side, nearly 200 feet above. To
make a short cut to the rest-house, the river must be
crossed, and as there is no bridge, there is usually
water to be waded through ; it comes nearly to the
hips, and a cool but wet passage is made, but as the
rest-house is close, fording is not a great drawback.
The baggage may be taken by another road. The view
from the outside of the rest-house is one of the most
striking to be seen, even in Kashmir. The first near
view is obtained of the great Pir Panjal range and the
pass. The mountains are very lofty, and look impassable ;
below is a lower range, and the tops of many hills are
seen. The river has a wide, stony bed, and during the
rains there is a powerful torrent. A fine old Mogu
serai was here, but it is now in ruins. Supplies are

plentiful, the cost of a good fat sheep is about Rs. 4. The spring near the rest-house is beautiful.

Changas Serai to Rajaori, 15 *miles.*—The road is level, but occasionally rough. It lies along the valley of the Tawi. The scenery is beautiful. The wide rich valleys are well cultivated ; the chief produce is wheat. The mountain torrents that run through the valleys are cleverly used for irrigating the fields. The cultivators live in square stone buildings, which are generally isolated. The river Tawi is here confined in a narrow bed, and its continuous roar is heard from the road. A mile before reaching Rajaori the river must again be forded, but early in the month of May there is not much difficulty ; later, in the rains, another road must be taken. Rajaori is only a very small place. Some centuries ago it was a royal residence, and the capital of a petty Rajah's territories. Later on the Moguls made the ruler a tributary ; finally the Sikhs, under Maharajah Golab Singh, took possession of the whole. Some of the in- habitants are reported to have left the country and to have settled in Central India. The rest-house is on the opposite side of the river to the town. It is situated in an old Mogul garden. It is a pavilion overlooking the river, and has a few rooms which travellers occupy. The town should be visited. There are some *samadhis* of Rajputs, and Mogul graves, also traces of a fine old Mogul serai, and at the other end of the town, an old mosque, which is still used Near it are some very old graves. On a head-stone, leaning against the wall, is an inscription in Persian, giving the name of a Munshi and the date of his death 300 years ago. Part of the second lower range of the Himalayas lies to the

south of Rajaori.   On the top of a hill near the rest-
house is a fort built by Maharajah Ranbir Singh.   It
is not completed, but has two or three guards, who
have a few old muskets, a sword, and some curious old
Sikh guns.   Part of the hill is cultivated.   The view
from the top is extensive.   Very often in July and
August the rest-house cannot be reached, but opposite
the town the red river may be crossed with some difficulty, and with the help of the *Thekdar*, shelter may be
had in the town itself.   If the floods have not subsided,
there is risk of life in fording the river, but, if urgency
requires it, by walking about two miles up the stream
on a narrow road, it may be crossed with less difficulty
and risk.   Before reaching Thanna Mundi, the next
stage, the river must again be twice forded.   There is
an alternate route, much used by the old Moguls,
from Rajaori to Aliabad Serai *via* Darhal pass (13,080
feet).   The distance by this route is 31 miles (three
stages).   The scenery is simply lovely.   The Nilasar
and the Nandansar lakes, two clear blue sheets of water,
are seen.   Supplies are, however, scarce, and instead of
rest-houses there are shepherds' huts.

Rajaori to Thanna Mundi, 14 *miles.*—This march brings
the traveller to the high range of mountains which encloses the valley of Kashmir.   The mountains are
loftier, and the valleys narrower and deeper as the Pir
Panjal pass is approached.   Its snow-capped top
rises grandly above every surrounding peak Near
Thanna Mundi is a fine old Mogul serai ; the entrance
gate is standing, and the greater part of the square,
the original form of the building.   There is a double
row of rooms, the walls are remarkably thick, and the

roof is a handsome specimen of Mogul architecture.
Several families occupy the rooms, which are blackened
by smoke, but in them the outlines of the Mogul designs may still be traced. At this serai are some stuffed
gold and silver pheasants and some Argus pheasants
shot in the mountains. The people are like the inhabitants of the valley of Kashmir. They dress in the
same way, and are fair. Some of the women have the
beautiful eyes of the true Kashmiris; their peculiar
dress—a long loose garment—however. hides the graceful beauty of their figures, but their lovely eyes cannot
fail to be noticed. The rest-house at Thanna Mundi
at the foot of the Rutton Pir, a huge round mountain
over 8,000 feet high, is like a barrack with a few sets of
rooms. Those who prefer to avoid the stiff ascent of
the next two or three marches, turn off here by the road
leading over part of the Rutton Pir to Poonch, and
thence to Baramulla and Srinagar.

Thanna Mundi to Baramgalli, 10 *miles.*—The ascent to
Rutton Pir commences immediately after leaving
Thanna Mundi. The road is steep and uncared for,
but not very difficult, though some parts try the climbing capacities of the ponies to the outmost. Rocks
have to be climbed over, and big stones, the surface
made smooth by the traffic. But the little " tats," if
left entirely to themselves, choose their footsteps carefully, and rarely make a false step. The view, as the
top of Rutton Pir is approached, is very charming
Quite new scenery, varying in extent, attracts the eye
from the big round sides of the mountain up which the
narrow road winds along. On the top are some huts,
near which the traveller will probably rest for break-

fast.   There is a fine spring of clear water close at
hand.   The air is cold, but the views are many and
beautiful, if the atmosphere is not, as is unfortunately
often the case, heavy and obscured.   Here is the
tomb of Rutton Pir Shah, a saint and a great traveller, who lived before the time of the Mogul Emperors.
The descent through a forest of deodars is gradual,
and continues till close to the village of Baramgalli.
Some of the deodars are very fine trees, but many of
these giants of the forests have fallen and been allowed to remain as they lie for many years.   Some of
the views from the top overlook the forest, the tall
straight battalions of deodars presenting a striking appearance.   Elms and other trees, some of them very
large, are also met ·with on the way down.   Near
the foot of the mountain flows a torrent, which
roars along over great boulders.   It is crossed by
a wooden bridge just before entering the plain on
which Baramgalli stands.   The bungalow here is
built near a big walnut tree, which affords a pleasant
shade.   The valley is small and almost entirely enclosed
by the mountains.   The few peasants, who live an isolated life here, tilling the little plots of level ground, often
crowd round the traveller asking for medicines.   They
will accept and drink any chemist's abomination grate-
fully.   From Baramgalli to Shupyan the weather cannot be depended upon, as clouds are attracted by the
lofty top of Pir Panjal.   Near the rest-house at Baramgalli is a waterfall of about 400 feet—one of the largest
in Kashmir.   It can be seen from the road when com-
mencing the next march.   Baramgalli is in the territory
of the Poonch Rajah.

Baramgalli to Poshiani, 10 *miles.*—The road on this march runs for some distance along a deep narrow valley, by the banks of a torrent, which has to be crossed several times over frail-looking wooden bridges Besides the big waterfall already mentioned, some smaller falls may be seen on this march. In the early part of the season the valley sometimes is full of snow, which has slipped down from the tops of the lower mountains. After a long march through the valley, a fertile plain is reached, and the ascent of the Pir Panjal really begins. The road is very steep, and full of big rocks difficult to climb over. This rough ascent continues till Poshiani is reached—a small collection of huts curiously perched on the side of the mountain. The few people who may be seen are not regular inhabitants. They come chiefly from Baramgalli about the middle of May to pasture their goats and cows, and remain only during the summer. The village seems to be placed on the top of a precipice, for the side of the mountain abruptly descends into a deep ravine far below. Snow may be seen on the top of the opposite mountains in the early season, and the path over the Pir Panjal pass may be distinctly traced, covered with snow, which also lies on the top of this range up to the month of June. There is no rest-house at Poshiani, but an unoccupied mud hut, capable of sleeping two or three, is built, like the rest of the village, on the side of the precipice. It is not dirty, but it is certainly not nice. A number of air-holes let in the cold winds from the snowy regions around. There is no spot level enough to pitch a tent on. If a traveller insists, he must pitch his tent on the top of the neighbouring mud

huts. The scenery during the march is beautiful.
The torrent, already referred to, is simply fascinating.
It has to be crossed and recrossed about 20 or 30 times
over wooden bridges of a rather primitive style. Some
of them are very shaky, and should not be crossed on
horse-back.

From Baramgalli there is another route to Srinagar,
via the Chchotagulli pass (14,092 feet), but it is very
difficult. There are no rest-houses, and supplies are
scarce. The distance covered is about 56 miles. The
traveller should be thoroughly well equipped with every
necessary.

There is no rest-house beyond Baramgalli on the Pir
Panjal route.

Poshiani to Aliabad Serai, 11 *miles.*—This is the great
march of the route ; for the Pir Panjal pass, about half
way, has to be crossed, and then commences the descent into the vale of Kashmir. If there is snow on the
pass, grass shoes (they cost one anna a pair) ought to
be worn. The wind will be found bitterly cold, and the
steep rough path before the pass is reached will have
ice hard frozen in several places. It is almost a
necessity to walk the distance, and a wet foot is certain,
for the grass shoes let in the snow readily, and an icy
chill runs through the feet. After about two and half
hours of marching the pass is reached, and the ascent
up the snow is very trying. It is a straight line to the
top over the hard snow worn smooth by traffic. Energy
and perseverance, however, have their reward, and
the traveller will find himself at the snow-clad top.
In the middle is the hut of a *fakir.* It is a wretched
place, this habitation of the holy man, and probably

covered with snow.   The *fakir* only lives here in the
summer, when the snow has melted.   If he attempted
to remain in the winter, he would certainly not see the
following summer, for his hut   would be his tomb.
Arrived   at   the   top,   some   disappointment will probably be felt at the magnificent view being dimmed
by the mists of the valleys beneath.   An hour should,
however, be spent enjoying the novelty of the situation,
even though the minarets of Lahore *musjid* may not
be seen, nor Rawalpindi either, as it is said they may
be in clear weather.   But the views are, nevertheless,
very grand, and by the help of a good binocular or
telescope, there is plenty to occupy full attention for
an hour.   In the opposite direction, there is nothing
but the tops of the mountains to be seen, but the
fine plateau through which the road leads from the
top down to Aliabad Serai, if covered with snow, is
a sight worth beholding.   Care should, however, be
taken to protect the eyes from the glare of the sun
on the snow, for cases of snow-blindness have occurred from exposure at this spot.   Coming up the mountain over the snow, the pass is shaded in the early
morning.   On this plateau, when free from snow, large
flocks of sheep and cattle are grazed in the summer
months.   Numerous streams of water will be met
rushing down the sides into the valleys below in noisy
torrents, and going to swell the rivers in the plains.
Aliabad Serai, three or four miles down the mountain,
is beautifully situated, but it is a cold and very comfortless place.   The rest-house is the old Mogul serai,
standing in a square. The old gateway remains, and
gives an appearance of comfort to the weary ; but in-

side, the old rooms with their three feet thick walls, without doors or windows, are as comfortless as can be imagined. When rain is falling, as is so often the case, fires should be lighted and kept up all night. The supplies are limited. The temperature is low. On 17th May, 1882, the thermometer stood at 45° in the shade at two o'clock in the afternoon. There is a tombstone here over the grave of a surgeon, who died at the serai from cholera in 1876, on his way back from Kash·mir, where he had been for a few months during an outbreak of cholera. It is about 50 yards in front of the serai on a little plain. The spot is well chosen. The traveller would do well to provide himself with a light hill tent for this journey. The mud huts on the top of the Pir Panjal pass are often used by coolies during the night, and are very dirty, and the serai at Aliabad may quite rightly be termed unfit for human habitation.

Aliabad Serai to Hirpura, 12 miles.—This march is very delightful, and the views on the way down are magnificent. The whole range of mountains encircling the valley may be seen in the early season covered with snow down to 3,000 feet, peaks from 15,000 feet to 18,000 feet towering up here and there, gleaming in their mantle of spotless white. The road for some distance is steep and very precipitous. There is a spot, between two and three miles from the rest-house, where two hundred years ago three or four elephants carrying the ladies of the Emperor Aurangzebe's harem, fell down the precipice about 1,000 feet. Ladies and elephants were all killed. This horrible accident arose from the rotten state of the road. A stone wall now

protects the side, but to this day the same spot is dangerous, and is in constant want of repairs. The difficulty
of keeping the road long in good order arises from the
fact that it is always slipping away owing to the constant rain. Hirpura is in a lovely valley, part of the
vale of Kashmir, beautifully wooded. It is said to
rain here daily the greater part of the year. There
are two rest-houses occupying the opposite sides of a
square. The new one was built by the present Maharajah,
and is in the usual barrack form. It is not water-tight,
and unless the roof has been recently repaired, is not a
comfortable residence in wet weather. The rest-house
opposite is the ruin of an old Mogul serai. The lower
part is used as a stable, and the long low room on the
upper floor is not exactly redolent of the perfumes of
Arabia. It is, however, water-tight, and the traveller,
in case rain is falling and he has not brought a tent,
would do well to sleep over the stable in preference to
using the barracks.

Hirpura to Shupyan, 9 *miles.*--In this march the valley
of Kashmir is fairly entered. The road is a regular
descent through a park-like country. On the green
sward may be seen several English flowers, among
which the forget-me-not is found in abundance. The
scenery around is altogether English, except for the
circle of lofty mountains, covered with snow in the
early part of the season, which impart a sense of
novelty purely Kashmirian. A number of torrents
rush sparkling along the little valleys, the land is
covered with rich crops, and there is an entire change
from the grandeur of the mountains, over which the last
few marches have been made, to the soft scenes in the

valleys. Shupyan, which may be designated a town, the only one on the south side of the Jhelum, is on the bank of a wide mountain torrent, which, but for being kept in control by embankments, would cover the whole country around with water. Opposite the rest-house, a barrack, are some plane trees, not very large, but interesting, as some of the first of these trees, so many of which, but generally much larger, are found in those other parts of the vale to which the traveller is slowly marching.

There is a pleasant day's excursion to be made here to the waterfall, or rather cataract, at Haribal, about seven miles distant. It is the source of the river Veshan, an important tributary of the Jhelum, into the left bank of which it falls a little below Kambal, opposite a village called Marbama. Starting from the rest-house at Shupyan, the march is over a fine table-land, rather wild and something like a "common" in England, with similar furze-bushes, buttercups, and forget-me-nots. Dozens of larks rise singing high into the air in all directions, pleasing all ears with their beautiful song. The village of Sedan is about five miles from Shupyan. It is very prettily situated on the Veshan, close to the mountain. Haribal is about three miles further on. A guide may be taken here, for the road is unfrequented, and lies up the side of the mountain, at times very difficult marching. After toiling up for about 1,000 feet, the noise of falling water will be heard, but the cataract is not visible. When the roar sounds near, a huge rock is seen. The guide then gives instructions to the visitors to go on their hands and knees for a few feet, and then throw themselves flat down on the bare rock Following the example of the guide, each person will, in this position, stretch out his hand, and catch hold of the edge of the rock. Then slowly drawing himself to the edge he will peer over. Then only can the cataract be seen about five hundred feet below. The fall of water is about 300 feet, and a great volume of spray is thrown up. The water may be seen eddying round in the deep rocky billow beneath till it falls again into the narrow channel, and then makes its way in tortuous windings as far as the eye can see in the wide beautiful plain lying stretched out below. Returning from this new sensation the traveller will notice the many fruit-trees, cherry, pear, and apple, growing wild on the road, and he probably will also notice the wild strawberries and raspberries. A jackal or two may be met on the way. A leopard occasionally makes his presence in the vicinity manifest by killing a goat or a sheep in his rounds at night. In the town of Shupyan there is not much to be seen. The houses here, and particularly at the village of Sedan, are not quite built in the usual Kashmiri style, but have a Swiss cottage-like appearance, affording a pleasing variety. There is a wooden mosque here which is a good specimen of the Kashmir style of architecture in these buildings. A State dispensary is located at Shupyan

Shupyan to Ramoo, 11 *miles.*—The march lies along flat country the whole of the way, with diversions through woods and shady spots. About seven miles from Shupyan, in an open place, is a curious collection of stones of various shapes. The story told by the people hereabouts is that some centuries ago a *fakir* was killed during the celebration of a wedding. Why the crime was committed the story says not, but it is affirmed that the *fakir* in his dying moments prayed that the whole party might be turned into stone. The prayer was granted, and hence these curious-looking stones on the plain. As evidence of the truth of the story, the bride's *duhli*, the bodies of the horses in the procession, and some of the persons present are shown. No resemblance can be traced in the stones to the bodies of men or brutes, but the *duhli* is certainly there. The material looks more like hardly-baked clay than stone, but the relics are curious, and one might almost suppose them to record an event of some kind, perhaps the destruction of the bride and some of the party by lightning. Several of the stones look like Muhammadan grave-stones, and there is an inscription in Persian on one or two of them.

There is no rest-house at Ramoo, but the traveller's servants can find shelter in the Native *dharmsala*. The village lies partly on the side of a hill, on the top of which is a cultivated plateau, from whence an extensive view may be had of the country round, with Srinagar in the distance, lying at the foot of Tukht-i-Suleiman and the fort, both of which are clearly visible.

Ramoo to Srinagar, 18 *miles*.—This is a long but easy march. It may be divided by stopping at Wahtor, about half way, and pitching a tent under some noble plane trees, close to the village. This arrangement will be found advantageous, as it enables the traveller to reach Srinagar in a short march, at an earlier hour than he otherwise could, and without being much fatigued. Some walking about in Srinagar will be needful probably before a suitable spot can be selected at which to pitch one's tent. The road from Wahtor

is perfectly level, and it terminates with the novelty,
for Kashmir, of a well-kept road. On each side are
poplar trees, 25 feet apart, reaching the whole way from
Wahtor to Srinagar. Some fine chinar trees will also
be seen. Many of the older trees are hollow, and the
inhabitants have in all cases enlarged the hollows by
cutting pieces of firewood from the sides—a custom
very often tending to the destruction of the trees. The
small river Dudhganga is met with on this march.
It rises in the mountains not far from Ramoo, and flows
into the Jhelum at the farther end of Srinagar. Just
before entering the capital is to be seen a Hindu temple, in a large enclosure, in the centre of which is the
samadhi of the Emperor Golab Singh.

THE POONCH ROUTE.
Thanna Mundi to Baramulla.

The marches from Gujrat to Thanna Mundi, which
travellers by the Poonch route must make, have been
described above. The following is a list of the marches
and distances after leaving Thanna Mundi.

No.	Names of places.	Distance in miles.	Remarks.
8	Gujrat to Thanna Mundi ..	97½	See Pir Panjal route.
9	Sooran	16	Rest-house.
10	Poonch	14	Rest-house. Supplies abundant.
11	Kahoota ...	10	Rest-house. Supplies difficult to obtain.
12	Aliabad	8	No rest-house. No supplies.
13	Hydrabad ...	7	No rest-house. No supplies. Snow over Haji Pir till middle of May.
14	Uri	10	Joins Jhelum valley road.

The marches on this route are difficult, there are two
more than by that of the Pir Panjal. The road is bad
and mountainous, and supplies are not abundant;
whereas the last three marches on the Pir Panjal
route are in the valley of Kashmir.   Presuming that
this Poonch route is chosen, the marches continue in the
order noted.

Thanna Mundi to Sooran, 16 *miles.*—A slight ascent leads
after six miles to the pass over the Rutton Pir, thence
the descent is easy ; forests on the sides of the mountain
and in the deep valley below afford shade and varied
views.   A stream in the valley is crossed many times.
Soon after the Sooran river must be forded, and then
the road follows the valley, and is comparatively level.
The rest-house contains four rooms.

Sooran to Poonch, 14 *miles.*—The valley of the Sooran
is followed the whole way ; the river is crossed close to
the village.   About half way a considerable stream is
passed ; near it is a path over the mountains to Gulmarg.   Poonch, the chief town in the Poonch territory,
hardly deserves to be called a town.   It is on the
right bank of the Sooran, which falls into a large river
called the Bitarh, a little below the town on the west.
The palace occupied by Rajah Baldeo Singh is notice-
able, and also the new fort.   The rest-house here is
a better and more commodious building than the one
at Sooran.

Poonch to Kahoota, 9 *miles.*—The road on this march
passes through a cultivated valley, near the bank of the
Bitarh.   Kahoota is a very small village ; it lies at the
foot of a range of hills, at a slight elevation above the
bank of the river.   The rest-house stands by itself in

open ground, and, on account, perhaps, of only occasional visitors, is a very small building. Supplies are
not plentiful here or at the other rest-houses.

Kahoota to Aliabad, 8 *miles*.—The road for three miles
is in a valley, and then descends between rocks to the
bed of a mountain torrent, which must be forded. For
the rest of the way the road is difficult and rough.
Aliabad is a collection of huts on the side of the hill,
and the march is terminated by the Haji Pir range,
which is crossed in the succeeding march.

Aliabad to Hydrabad, 7 *miles*.—This march is also a short
one. The road runs nearly straight up the mountain
for three miles over the Haji Pir pass, and in a similar
manner descends on the opposite side, but through
dense forests. The elevation of this pass is about 8,500
feet. At the top there is a *fakir's* hut, and grass grows
luxuriantly. Hydrabad is another small village high on
the side of the mountain, but in Kashmir territory. The
dominions of the Rajah of Poonch are now passed.
There is no rest-house.

Hydrabad to Uri, 10 *miles*.—The road runs on the left
bank of a stream called the Shah Kakuta. The march
is rough and difficult, ascending and descending many
times, with an occasional stream to ford. Three or four
miles from Hydrabad one of the largest waterfalls in
Kashmir is to be seen. After the difficulties of this
march have been safely got over, the road joins the
Jhelum valley road.

CHAPTER III.

THE VALE OF KASHMIR.

THE territory of His Highness the Maharajah of Jammu and Kashmir extends from 32° 17′ to 36° 58′, north latitude, and from 73° 26′ to 80° 30′, east longitude. It covers an area of 80,900 square miles, with a population estimated in 1891 of 2,543,952 persons. It is bounded on the north by some petty semi-independent hill states, mostly subordinates to Kashmir, and by the Karakoram mountain and the Karakoram pass, the principal route between India and Turkestan. On the east by Chinese Tibet. On the south and west by the Punjab districts of Rawalpindi, Jhelum, Gujrat and Sialkote, and the Hazara country. The ruler of this extensive dominion is His Highness Major-General Maharajah Pratap Singh, G.C.S.I. Kashmir is a country with diverse races, who speak different languages, profess different religions, and have different customs and manners. For administrative purposes it is divided into two divisions, Jammu and Kashmir, which includes Ladakh, Skardu and Gilgit. The valley of Kashmir, which is entirely surrounded by lofty ranges of the Himalaya mountains, is about 84 miles in length, and 20 to 25 miles in breadth, covering an area of about 1,850 square miles. It is nearly in the centre of the Kashmir territory. The elevation of the valley is about 5,300 feet above sea level; it is traversed by the river Jhelum, which rises near Vernag at the

east end of the valley, and is navigable from Islamabad to Baramulla, nearly the entire length of the valley.
After receiving several tributary streams, it runs through
the gorge at Baramulla, a noisy and in some places a
deep narrow torrent through the mountains, till it
reaches the Punjab plains. There are several minor
valleys opening into the Kashmir valley. The principal of these are Lolab, Sind, Liddar, and Nohng.
In the surrounding hills there are several grassy valleys
and meadows; the principal are Gulmarg, Sonamarg,
Zojimarg, and Rupamarg. The *margs*, or mountain
downs, are numerous on the top of the hills below the
Pir Panjal, one of which, Gulmarg, is the summer resort of visitors to the valley. Some are found also on
the slopes of the mountains on the north-eastern sides
of the valley, one of which is the Sonamarg in the
Sind valley. These downs serve as grazing grounds
for herds of ponies, cattle, sheep and goats. The principal tributaries of the Jhelum are the Liddar, Sind,
Pohru, Vishan, Romush, Rambiara, and Dudhganga.
The lakes in the valley are the Dal or the City lake,
Anchar, Manesbal and Wular, the last being the largest.
There is a lower range of mountains, close to the higher range, within the valley, encircling it The land,
which on both sides of the river is very flat for several
miles, is used chiefly for the cultivation of rice. The
rest of the valley is composed of extensive table-lands
and sloping hills, which descend gradually from the
mountains into the plains. The plateaux are
known as *karewahs*, and are under cultivation. They
are supposed to have resulted from the gradual suhsi-
dence of the waters when the whole of the valley was

a vast lake. There are several lofty peaks among the mountains surrounding the valley. The highest in the Pir Panjal ranges are Muli, 14,952 feet above sea level, and Aheetotopa, 13,042 feet. In the north of the valley is Harmuk, 16,903 feet, a mountain sacred to the Hindu Goddess Parbatia, who from her mountain home on the Harmuk used to sail in her pleasure-boat on the great lake Satistar, which occupied the valley. Further south is Mahadev, and the peak of Amarnath, 17,321 feet. North of the valley is the Zojila pass (11,300 feet) leading to Leh. Near this pass towers the peak of Gwashbrari or Kolahoi, 17,839 feet. Then there is the Hoksar pass, 13,315 feet, leading to Petgam. The loftiest peak of all is Nanga Parbat in Chilas, to the north-west of Kashmir, 26,629 feet above sea level. There are several passes leading into the valley, the principal of which are, on the north Razdiangan (11,800 feet), and Burzil (13,600 feet) ; on the south Marbal (11,570 feet), Banhal (9,200 feet), and Pir Panjal (11,400 feet) ; on the east Margan (11,300 feet), Zojila (11,300 feet), and Karakoram (18,317 feet); on the west Tosa Maidan (10,560 feet); and on the north-west Nattishinar (10,200 feet).

The river Jhelum, Vitasta of the Hindus and Hydaspes of the Greeks, runs through the valley from east to west for about a hundred miles from its source at Vernag to Baramulla, where it narrows into a mountain torrent and is not navigable. The river falls 165 feet in the first 30 miles, and 55 feet in the next 25 miles to Wular, beyond which the fall is very slight. Before reaching Khanabal, one mile from Islamabad, three or four streams fall into it. The Sind river, nearly as large as the Jhelum, falls into it at Shadipore. The Jhelum is during the dry season a very inconsiderable river, but when the snow melts on the high mountains surrounding the valley in May, the waters are greatly swollen, causing great floods, which occasionally prove disastrous. Such a flood occurred in 1893, which swept away all the bridges, with the exception of the Amira Kadal. The magnificent bridge over the Jhelum at Domel, the dâk bungalow there, and the old suspension bridge at Kohala were completely destroyed. For several days eight feet of water ran over the Munshi Bagh. Below Sopur is the river Pohru, which runs down through part of the Lolab valley, and is only navigable during the summer months. The Dudhganga is a small stream which rises in the Pir Panjal range, and is first met with on the march from Ramoo to Srinagar, the last on the route. It falls into the Jhelum immediately below Srinagar. A little beyond, in the Tilail valley, rises the river Kishenganga. It contains a considerable volume of water, and flows in a north-westerly direction till near Shardi, where it turns to the south-west and flows into the Jhelum, just below Muzaffarabad. At the east end of the valley is the Wardwar river, which flows south through the valley of Maru Wadwan, and falls into the Chenab above Kishtwar.

There are several magnificent springs in the valley, such as Achhabal, Vernag, Kokarnag, Arpal and Chusma Sahi. Sulphurous springs exist at Wuyun near Pampor and at Islamabad, and it is believed that there are several hot springs in the Dal and Wular lakes.

ADMINISTRATION.

Kashmir is a province in the territories of His Highness the Maharajah of Jammu and Kashmir. For administrative purposes it includes the district of Muzaffarabad. The valley proper is divided into eleven *tahsils*, which are as follows :—1, Lal ; 2, Srinagar ; 3, Sri Pratap Singhpur ; 4, Nagam ; 5, Wantipura ; 6, Anantnag ; 7, Haripur ; 8, Sri Rangbir Singhpur ; 9, Uttur Manchipura ; 10, Sopur ; 11, Pattan. Each *tahsil* is controlled by a *tahsildar*. The head judicial officer of Kashmir is the Chief Judge, who hears appeals from the courts of all the subordinate judges in Srinagar, and also from the courts of *tahsildars*, who are both executive and judicial officers. The chief revenue officer is called the Hakim Ala or Governor. The above departments and such others as the police, settlement, education, medical, accounts, and forests are very well managed. The Postal and Telegraphic Departments are in the hands of the Imperial Government, but the telegraphic line from Srinagar to Jammu, *via* Banihal, and from Srinagar to Skardu are worked by the State Telegraph Department.

The Resident in Kashmir and his assistant have the power to enquire into or try cases against European British subjects, Americans, Europeans of any nationality other than British, Christians of European descent, Native Indian subjects, such subjects as are either merely visiting the territories of His Highness the Maharajah, or acting as servants of a European British subject, and British subjects accused of having committed offences conjointly with European British subjects. The trial of Native Indian subjects, who ordinarily dwell or carry on business or personally work for gain within the Kashmir territories, rests with the courts of the Darbar. The Resident and his assistant have also the power to dispose of suits in which (1) both parties are subjects of Her Majesty, not ordinarily dwelling or carrying on business within Kashmir territories; (2) the defendant is an European British subject; (3) the defendant is a Native Indian subject of Her Majesty, and at the time of the commencement of the suit does not ordinarily dwell or carry on business within the territories of the Maharajah. All other suits between British subjects on the one hand, and subjects of the Maharajah on the other, come before the courts of the State.

HISTORY.

The history of Kashmir may be divided into seven epochs—1, Pre-historic; 2, Hindu; 3, Muhammadan; 4, Mogul; 5, Durani; 6, Sikh; 7, Dogra.

The famous book " Rajtarangini," written by Kalhana Pandit, and subsequently continued by other writers, is the chief source of historical information about Kashmir. It is written in Sanskrit verse, and is composed of eight cantos. It has been translated by Mr. J. C. Dutt, of Calcutta, into English.

PRE-HISTORIC.

" Rajtarangini " commences with an account of the desiccation of the valley by Kashapa. At an early period the entire valley of Kashmir is supposed to have been a vast mountain lake, and the remains of fresh water fish found on the table-land, together with other

traces which may be seen on the sides of some of the
mountains, tend to confirm this view. Eventually the
pressure of water on the weakest point in the mountains, which would have been at Baramulla, forced a
passage there, and the vast body of water which was
let loose tore a way for itself through the mountains, till
the Punjab plains were reached. In returning from
Kashmir by the Murree route, the traveller may perceive
more readily than he would on entering Kashmir, a
number of deep indentations on the sides of the mountains. Some are semi-circular, where water has evidently either rushed through in a resistless torrent,
cleaving the side of the mountain, or where resistance
has been met with, has eddied round, cutting its way
through, till the pressure from behind being gradually
reduced, the water has finally been confined to
its present channel in the contracted bed of the
Jhelum.

This great lake was called Satisar, or the lake of Sati,
another name of the goddess Parvati. In it resided the
demon Zaludban, who preyed upon mankind. It
happened that Kashapa, son of Marichi, and grandson
of Brahma, visited the country, and inquired into the
cause of the distress of the people. When informed
of Zaludban and his cruelty, Kashapa passed a thousand
years in austere devotion, and invoked the aid of the
gods, who, opening the mountain at Baramulla, drained
off the lake and slew Zaludban. The name of Kashmir
may possibly be derived from this event, being a con-
traction of Kashapmar, or the country of Kashap. Or
the derivation may be from two Sanskrit words *kas mira*,
water drained.

HINDU PERIOD.

In the early period of Hindu history, there was a patriarchal form of Government, and subsequently the headman of each village, the Kota Rajah, was the nominal king. Naturally these kings constantly quarrelled with one another, and the people, exasperated by the anarchy which prevailed, called a Rajput from the Jammu country to rule over them. The hill rajah, Dayakaran, settled in Kashmir, and it is said that for a period of 633 years, fifty-five of his descendants reigned in Kashmir. The last of this dynasty was Somadat, who was killed in the battle between Kuras and Pandus, celebrated in the Mahabharata. After Somadat's death, Gouanda became king. He ascended the throne in 3121 B.C. According to Kalhana, in 2448 B.C. Several dynasties followed. During this period Raja Ramdev built the famous temple on the plateau of Mattan, about 3007 B.C. King Lau built a city at Lolah, and Wazir Bambro took the kingdom from King Prahlad. A popular song among the Kashmiris tells of the loves of Bambro and a beautiful woman named Lolare. The song is known as *Lolare Bambro*. Asoka conquered Kashmir in about 1394 B.C. He introduced Buddhism, but his son, Jaloka, renounced his father's faith and established the Shiva form of worship. Another name which figures in the history of Kashmir of this period is Sandeman, who placed on the throne three princes of Turkestan,—Hushk, Zushk, and Kanishk—who ruled for 41 years. A succeeding rajah, Abhimanyu, uprooted Buddhism in Kashmir. Mehrakul is remembered as a powerful but cruel king. Gopaditya was the sixth king after Mehrakul, and built the temple on the Tukht-i-Suleiman.

Raja Pravarsen founded the city of Srinagar. Lalita-
ditya reigned from 697 to 738 A.D. He was just and
enlightened, and under his rule the people prospered.
Full details of the history of the country under the
kings who followed him are to be found in the " Rajtarangini." Queen Dida, wife of Khemagupta, ruled 23 years,
and it is said that she murdered her own grandsons in
order to assume the reins of Government. The Hindu
kingdom ended in the early part of the 14th century.
From all accounts, it appears that the people were
happy under the Hindu kings, who ruled with justice
tempered with mercy. Various public works in the
nature of canals and great buildings, some of which
still remain, are proof of the prosperity of their Raj.

MUHAMMADAN PERIOD.

This period commences with the reign of Renchan
Shah, who was a son of the King of Tibet. Coming
as an adventurer to the valley, he was attached to the
court of Sahadiv, in whose reign Zulfikadr Khan, the
Tartar, invaded Kashmir. Renchan Shah was married
to Kuta Rani, daughter of Ram Chund, the commander-
in-chief. He proclaimed himself king in 1323 A.D.
He wanted to become a Hindu, but the Brahmans
refused to admit him into the faith. They were probably sorry for this afterwards, for there came a Sayyid,
named Bulbul Shah, from Arabia, who made the king a
convert to Islam. Renchan changed his name to
Sadruddin, killed many Hindus, and destroyed their
temples and scriptures. In his time the universal cry
was " *Na batu ham* "—" I am not a Hindu." Renchan
rebuilt the Juma *masjid*, which had been burnt down,

and the Bulbullankar. After his death, Udayandev, brother of Sahadeva, married his widow and reigned 15 years. After the latter's death, Shah Mirza, the commander-in-chief under Kuta Rani, declared himself king. He proposed marriage to Kuta Rani, to which she consented, but soon afterwards stabbed herself to death. Shah Mirza then became king of Kashmir. Twenty-six Muhammadan kings followed. Of these Sultan Sikandar, called But-Shikan, or the Iconoclast, was notorious for his religious fanaticism, displayed in the destruction of Hindu temples. He demolished Martund and the temples of Avantipore and Pandritan. It is stated that he kept a large number of men in his service, whose sole duty it was to demolish temples and idols. A local story is to the effect that when he destroyed the image of Ganesh at Ganeshbal on the Amar Nath road, a stream of blood poured into the Liddar river. The Brahmans say that when the porch of the Bijbihara temple was being pulled down, a stone was found with the following inscription :

" *Bismilla mantrina nashante Vizaeshwari* "—" Bismilla is a magic word that will destroy the Vizaeshwari temple."

When this story was told the brutal Sikandar, he expressed his regret that by his actions he had fulfilled the predictions of idolators. He destroyed all the Sanskrit books he could lay hands on, and by force converted a number of Brahmans to Islam. Better days dawned on Kashmir with the reign of Zainulabdin, which commenced in 1417 A.D. He reigned for 52 years, and is still remembered by the Kashmiris as the great,

enlightened, tolerant, and virtuous Badshah. He
introduced the manufacture of the famous Kashmir
shawl by importing wool from Tibet and workmen
from Turkestan. He also taught the manufacture of
paper and *papier maché*—manufactures which exist to the
present day. Among other works of public utility, he
constructed the Nalla Mar canal between the city and
the Dal lake. He was a patron of literature, a poet,
and a great lover of field sports. Soon after his death
all the advantages gained by his benign rule were lost,
owing to the increasing influence of the clan of *Chaks*,
who raised themselves into power. They resisted for a
time attacks from without, but eventually jealousies
arose amongst themselves, and treachery and crime
destroyed their power. The *Chak* kings, who were
eight in number, reigned from 1554 to 1587 A.D.

In Yusuf Khan's reign a Mogul army, sent by the
Emperor Akbar, invaded Kashmir, but was routed
by Yakub Khan, the son of Yusuf Khan. The
victorious general, elated by his victory, became very
cruel to the Hindus and Sunis. The oppressed people
appealed to Akbar, who, during the years 1585 and
1587, despatched several expeditions into Kashmir.
The last army utterly defeated Yakub Khan, and
the Mogul rule was finally established in the country.

MOGUL PERIOD.

Kashmir had its share of the benefits of the rule of
the Emperor Akbar. He visited the valley three
times. During his reign Todarmal, the great financier,
made a revenue settlement of the country. The wall
round Hariparbat was built by Akbar. Then followed

Jehangir, during whose reign the numerous pleasure gardens in different parts of Kashmir were constructed. During the Mogul period the country was governed by Subadars, responsible only to the Emperor. Aititad Khan is remembered as a cruel ruler, while Jafar Khan and Ali Mardan Khan are spoken of as kind and just. The evil influence of Aurangzebe's reign was also felt in Kashmir, and never had the Hindus been so mercilessly persecuted. With the decay of the Mogul Empire, the Subadar assumed independent powers, and the country fell into anarchy. It was at this time that the Pathans invaded Kashmir and became its rulers.

DURANI PERIOD.

The Pathan rule commenced in 1752 A.D. with Ahmed Shah, the Afghan. Twenty-eight Durani rulers reigned in Kashmir from 1753 to 1819 A.D. It was fortunate for the country that the Pathan rule lasted no longer, for the oppression of the people, especially the Hindus, by these savages is perhaps unparalleled in the history of the world. During the rule of Jabbar Khan (1819), the last of the Durani kings, Ranjit Singh, the "Lion of the Punjab," had already become famous. A Pathan noble, Fatteh Khan Barakzai, promised to help the latter if he would invade Kashmir. The Sikh invasion would probably not have been successful had not Ranjit Singh been aided by the advice of a Kashmiri Pandit, Birbal Dal, who had fled to Lahore. While the Pandit was away at Lahore, attempting to rescue his country from the oppression of the Pathans, they were taking revenge by forcibly converting his family and zenana to Islam. His son's wife was made a Mussal-

mani and sent to Kabul, and Birbal's wife committed
suicide. The Pathan ruler, Muhammad Azim,
however, soon fled to Kabul, and in 1819 Ranjit
Singh's general, Misr Diwan Chand, planted the Sikh
flag on the fort of Hariparbat.

SIKH PERIOD.

The Sikhs ruled Kashmir through a Governor, deputed from Lahore. There were ten in all of these
governors. The rule of most was uneventful. Moti Ram
is remembered as a just man, and Kripa Ram as a
pleasure hunting and idle Governor. Colonel Mian
Singh, who was murdered at Srinagar by muti-
neers of the Sikh army, is spoken of as an enlightened
ruler, who introduced several reforms into the adminis-
tration. The mutiny was subdued by Ranjit Singh's
general, Gulab Singh. An account of Kashmir during
Colonel Mian Singh's governorship will be found in
Baron Hugel's and Vigne's books.

DOGRA PERIOD.

In 1845, during the governorship of Shekh Imamuddin, what is known as the second Sikh war broke
out, and after the battle of Subraon in 1846, Maharajah Gulab Singh, as minister of the Khalsa,
negotiated with the British at Amritsar, and the
Government of India transferred and made over for
ever in independent possession to the Maharajah and
heirs male of his body, all the hilly and mountainous
country situated to the east of the Indus and west of
the Ravi rivers. In consideration of this transfer,
Maharajah Gulab Singh paid to the British Govern·
ment the sum of 75 lakhs of rupees.

Imamuddin raised some opposition to the new ruler, but was soon disposed of by the great Sikh General. During the mutiny the latter sent a contingent of troops and artillery to co-operate with the English force at Delhi. In the same year he died, and was succeeded by his son, Maharajah Ranbir Singh, G.C.S.I., who was born in 1832. In the Afghan war of 1881, the latter also sent a contingent of troops and artillery to Lahore to assist the British Government, if required. They were reviewed, together with the troops sent from other Native States of India, at Lahore by Lord Lytton, .and a portion was sent to guard the country about the Khyber pass. The Maharajah received a *Sunnad* giving adoptive rights. He was a G.C.S.I. and C.I.E., a General in the British Army and Councillor of the Empress. He died in September, 1885, and was succeeded by his eldest son, Maharajah Pratap•Singh, G.C.S.I., Major-General in the British Army. He is now the Sovereign of Kashmir.

CLIMATE AND METEOROLOGY.

The climate of Kashmir is very salubrious and differs in many respects from that of the surrounding countries. As a sanitarium, Kashmir is well suited to those whose constitution is injured by the heat of the plains. The spring usually commences in the middle of March, when the fruit trees blossom and Nature assumes a glorious aspect. The spring is, however, cold, windy, and showery. In the middle of May summer begins, when the days are hot, but the nights cool. The heat increases in June, but it never becomes oppressive.

July and August are the hottest months, but frequent thunder storms in the evening have the effect of cooling the air.

During July and August, Srinagar and its outskirts are slightly malarious. In July heavy rain often pours for days, which, with the melting of the snow on the higher mountains, often produces floods. This rain is simultaneous with the south-west monsoon. Srinagar is, therefore, by no means a pleasant place to live in from the middle of June until the end of August. A most charming climate is available within a few hours' journey at Gulmarg, or at Gures, Sonamarg, Nagamarg, Nilamarg, Gogjipathar, etc.

September, October and November are dry months. October, with its fine crisp morning air, is the best month in Kashmir. The days are bright and sunny, and a more perfect climate cannot be imagined. At the end of October, snow falls on the higher mountains. November and December are very cold; in December snow falls in the valley. The nights are frosty in the middle of November, and by the end of that month the trees are stripped of their leaves, and the year's vegetation is killed off. Snow falls frequently in January and February, and the valley is usually covered with a white mantle during these two months. Severe frost, lasting for several days, often appears by the end of January. In some years it is so severe that the lakes and water-courses are frozen. Kashmir has good winter rainfall from December to March. In March the snow disappears and spring comes on with a burst. Kashmir is cooler than any of the other hill stations throughout the year, except in the months of June, July and

August. The exceptional cold in winter is probably accounted for by the fact that the valley is a closed hollow basin surrounded by high mountains. The most interesting feature of the climate is the large amount of sunshine combined with a low temperature. Such a climate, it is needless to say, is of the greatest value to consumptive and other patients. The winter is, however, not suited to persons suffering from chest diseases, rheumatism, or gouty diathesis. Purpura sometimes breaks out in epidemic form in Srinagar and the surrounding villages. Small-pox also is liable to be prevalent in the autumn.

The following meteorological table for 1895 will be of interest :—

Mhs.	Mean pressure during the month.	Date.	Highest pressure during the month.	Date.	Lowest pressure during the month.	Mean.	Mean maximum.	Mean minimum.	Highest temperature during the month.	Date.	Lowest temperature during the month.	Date.	Mean velocity of wind in miles per hour.	Mean humidity of hygrometer.	Mean of cloud proportions.	Total rainfall during the month.	Snowfall.
January	25·019	28	25·202	21	24·794	26·0	88·6	21·8	41·4	22	10·1	14	3·9	90	9·8	5·84	5·56
February	2071	21	25·244	2	24·759	23·1	83·0	18·5	44·0	20	-8·9	6	2·2	79	5·2	4·81	8·96
March	24·985	5	25·219	24	24·698	38·0	45·1	34·2	61·4	22	22·1	1	4·1	85	6·6	5·30	1·15
April	24·908	17	25·042	27	24·781	43·5	59·4	37·0	70·7	28	28·0	6	6·0	83	8·5	2·68	:
May	24·864	4	24·988	28	24·732	62·4	80·8	54·2	87·8	24	46·7	4	6·7	80	1·8	1·55	:
June	24·758	8	24·888	27	24·658	68·2	83·9	60·9	93·4	25	53·7	30	6·8	80	4·2	2·10	:
July	24·695	13	24·911	28	24·572	69·0	82·6	61·8	92·4	28	58·2	12	5·7	84	3·4	1·24	:
August	24·666	28	24·772	5	24·539	69·9	83·7	63·5	88·3	8	54·7	18	5·8	85	5·1	1·65	:
September	24·805	18	24·910	18	24·708	62·3	81·0	53·6	85·3	1	45·7	30	5·2	86	2·0	0·68	:
October	24·934	22	25·066	19	24·816	46·6	72·5	39·1	80·8	1	29·6	31	5·0	89	1·7	2·01	:
November	25·036	18	25·182	12	24·860	37·3	58·6	38·1	70·8	2	24·1	18	5·2	93	5·2	0·64	·57
December	25·019		25·200		24·806	32·2	48·5	29·1	52·5	2	22·1	8	4·3	94	8·0	0·62	
Sum	8763	:	300·624	:	296·723	578·5	757·2	506·8	808·8	:	398·4	:	58·9	1,028	56·5	29·02	11·24
Mn	24·897	:	25·052	:	24·725	48·2	63·1	42·2	72·4	:	33·2	:	4·0	85	4·7	2·42	·94

PEOPLE.

The inhabitants of Kashmir are of a primitive Aryan stock, who migrated from the Punjab at different times. They are sometimes fair and ruddy. The men are physically well-built and often very fine-looking. The women are sometimes very handsome. The *parda-nashins* are, of course, very rarely seen. The men wear a long shirt called *firan*, which in the case of Hindus has long, narrow sleeves, and Muhammadans short, full ones. The Hindu woman or Punditani wears a girdle and has a white cap, whereas the Mussulmani wears a red head-dress.. The black hair of young girls is braided in many thin strands, covering the back and forming a semi-circle, with a knot of hair hanging down the back, and stretching sometimes nearly to the feet. The Kashmiris are a great tea drinking nation, but as a rule they abstain from wine. Speaking of Kashmiri villagers, Mr. Lawrence, than whom there is no greater authority, says:—" If one looks to the purely material condition of the villagers, I should say that the Kashmiri peasant is in every respect better off than his fellows in India. He has ample food, sufficient clothing, a comfortable house, and abundance of fuel, and he obtains these without much effort."

The people of Kashmir before the fourteenth century were all Hindus. The mass of the people were forcibly converted to Islam by their Muhammadan rulers. The religious taxes and Mussalmani fanaticism induced many Hindus to fly out of the country and settle in India, where they now form a very intelligent section of the community. The Hindus of Kashmir are all

Brahmans, and are called Pandits. The Muhammadans, who form the bulk of the population, are divided into Shias and Sunnis, the former numbering about five per cent. of the total Muhammadan population. A sprink-ling of Sikhs, Rajputs, Moguls and Pathans is also to be found. There are many of the lower castes and sects, such as Dums, Galwans, Chanpans, and Watals. That the Muhammadans in Kashmir are the descendants of Hindus converted to Islam is corrobo-rated by the fact that the members of the two religions live on very amicable terms, and that the Muhammadans have not the same religious zeal that characterizes their co-religionists elsewhere. Many Muhammadans, too, still bear Hindu surnames, such as Rishi, Bat, and Pandit. It is also a singular fact that there are many places of worship which are held in reverence by both Hindus and Muham-madans.

The Kashmiris are an intelligent race, of a cheery and humorous, if somewhat imaginative, disposi-tion. Want of education and a succession of alien and oppressive rulers have no doubt degraded their character, but of late the spread of education, contact with other nations, and a better form of Government, are raising them to a higher and more civilised stage. Sir Lepel Griffin, writing of Kash-mir, says:—" For there, as part of the natural beauty in which they were born and nourished, an interesting race, an ancient and stately civilization, and a scientific religion, had their home long before Romulus traced with a furrow the future walls of Rome."

The census of 1891 showed a population for Kashmir, including Muzaffarabad, of 949,041 people, who
were thus classified—

Hindus. Sikhs. Muhammadans. Christians. Parsis.
  60,316   5,473   883,099   145   8

Males 502,345
Females 446,696

LANGUAGE.

The Kashmiris speak a distinct language, which has
been described as being " rather curiously and closely
related to the Sanskrit," but there are more Persian
than Sanskrit words in the Kashmiri language. Out of
100 words 40 will be Persian, 25 Sanskrit, 15 Urdu,
10 Arabic, and the remaining 10 Tibetan, Turki,
Dogri, or Punjabi. The language is not written, and is
rather difficult for a foreigner. The vocabulary is
rich, and there are many witty Kashmiri proverbs.
Hindustani is understood in Srinagar, and by persons
of position. The villagers speak and understand
nothing but Kashmiri. The court language is Persian,
although Urdu has also recently been introduced. In
former times Sanskrit was the universal medium of education, and many of the Pandits were great Sanskrit
scholars. There are many valuable Sanskrit manuscripts
still to be found in Kashmir, which are not obtainable
elsewhere. At the present day Persian is taught everywhere, and every educated man can speak that language
fluently. English is also now taught in some of the
schools, and future generations will probably be taught
entirely in the Western tongue. The study of history
is a favourite one, and almost every Kashmiri knows

something of the past of his country. Hindu astrology is very popular.

RELIGION.

The people of Kashmir were originally Nag worshippers, and then Pouranic Hinduism was the universal creed. There are in the valley of Kashmir a great number of springs, rushing from beneath the mountains, as though coming direct from the centre of the earth. To these a mysterious origin has been attributed from time immemorial by the inhabitants; on this account they have been dedicated by the former serpent-worshippers of Kashmir to the " Nag " or snake, the oldest form of worship. Sometimes a huge snake is believed to have its abode in the neighbouring mountain. The principal of these " Nags " are Kousar Nag, at the east end of the valley, at the top of a mountain in the Pir Panjal range; Shushi Nag, on the road to Amarnath; Anant Nag, Salik Nag, and Malak Nag in the town of Islamabad; Vernag, the chief source of the river Jhelum; Kukar Nag, also in the eastern part of the valley; and Gangabal in the Sind valley. Again, at Wuyun, there is a sulphur and iron stream of water, which is called Phaka Nag. A fresh-water spring near it is called Kalish Nag; a few miles beyond is another spring, at the foot of a mountain, in which the people of the village say there is a serpent still. There is a round building in a tank for him to occupy whenever he may feel disposed to leave the mountain. The name " Nag " given to these places is evidence of the ancient religion of the people of Kashmir, who may have belonged to the Scythian migration into Northern India about the sixth century before the Christian era. They were called **Takkas or Takshaks**, and they penetrated far into plains of the Punjab. Takshaka, or Taxila, the Punjab capital, was the largest city which Alexander the Great found between the Indus and the Jhelum, 327 B.C. The Scythic Takshaks are supposed to have been the source of the great serpent race, the **Takshakas or Nagas**, of whom so much is told in Sanskrit writings, and whose name is still borne by the Naga tribes at the extreme north-east of India. Naga and Takshaka in Sanskrit both mean a snake or tailed monster. We learn from Dr. Hunter's article on " India " in the " Imperial Gazetteer,"—" The Takshaks and Nagas were the tree and serpent worshippers, whose rites and objects of adoration have impressed themselves deeply on the architecture and sculptures of India. The names were applied in a confused manner to different races of Scythic origin. The Chinese records give a full account of the Naga geography of ancient India. The Naga kingdoms were both numerous and powerful, and Buddhism derived many of its royal converts from them. The Chinese chroniclers, indeed, classify the Naga princes of India into two great divisions, as Buddhists and non-Buddhists. The serpent-worship, which formed so typical a characteristic of the Indo-Scythic races, led the Chinese to confound them with the objects of their adorations; and the Indo-Scythic Nagas would almost seem to be the originals of the Dragon races of Chinese Buddhism and Chinese art." A learned writer remarks :—" No superstition was more deeply embedded in the ancient Hindu mind than reverence for Nagas or dragons. Buddhism from the

first had to contend as much against the under current
of Naga reverence in the popular mind as against the
superstitious opposition of the philosophic Brahman in
the upper current. At last, as it would seem, driven to
an extremity by the gathering cloud of persecution, the
Buddhists sought escape by closing with the popular
creed, and endeavouring to enlist the people against the
priests; but with no further success than such a respite
as might be included within some one hundred years."
It has already been stated that the Hindus of Kashmir
are all Brahmans. On this peculiarity Mr. Growse, in
his book " Mathura, a District Memoir," makes the
following remarks in the chapter on " Indian Caste:"
" In the genuine Veda there was no mention of caste
whatever, nor was it possible that there should be, on
the hypothesis now to be advanced, that the institution
of caste was the simple result of residence in a conquered country. This is confirmed by observing that
in the valley, which was one of the original homes of
the Aryan race, and was for many ages secured by its
position from foreign aggression, there is to the present
time no distinction of caste." In this connection the
following translation from the " Mahabharat " is interesting :—" There is no distinction of castes. The whole
of this world is Brahmanical, as originally created by
Brahma. It is only in consequence of men's actions
that it has come into a state of caste divisions."
Muhammadanism, as pointed out before, was introduced
in the 14th century. Kashmir Hindus are chiefly
Sivaites or worshippers of Siva and Parbati. There are
several places in the valley held sacred by the Hindus,
The spring of Khir Bhawani at the mouth of the Sind

valley, the water of which is said to change colour at intervals, is held in great veneration. Sharka Devi on the Hariparbat, Jwala Mukhi at Khriv, Bhawan, and Gangabal are also held sacred. But the great place for Hindu pilgrimage is the cave of Amarnath up the Liddar valley, where thousands of devout Hindus from all parts of India march up a most difficult road to be present on the full moon of the native month Sawan. The physical conditions of Kashmir often produce some curious natural phenomena, which may, in the majority of cases, be easily explained. The natives, however, regard the places where these phenomena occur as holy, and hold them in great veneration.

The Muhammadans of Kashmir are peculiarly superstitious. They are saint-worshippers. A crew of boatmen, when paddling, often invoke " Shukur-uddin, Nurdin," their patron saints, or pray to Dastgir. Shah-i-Hamadan, Makdum Sahib, Hazratbal, Juma *masjid*, and Dastgir are the principal *ziarats* in Srinagar, while the shrine of Nurdin at Chrar is held in peculiar reverence.

TRADE.

The Jhelum valley cart-road has given great impetus to trade in Kashmir. The country is self-contained, the valley providing all the necessaries of life, with the exception of salt. Surrounded by high mountains and being difficult of access, Kashmir might have continued for centuries without any contact with the outer world. At one time shawls were largely exported, and the trade gave employment to 25,000 men, and exceeded 30 lakhs in value annually. The industry is, however, now almost a thing of the past, the Franco-German war having given it a blow from which it never recovered. The articles at present exported from Kashmir are chiefly fruits, drugs, leather, ghee, timber, and woollen goods. The imports are chiefly cotton piecegoods, metals, salt, sugar, tea, and petroleum.

ARTS AND MANUFACTURES.

Kashmir is celebrated for several artistic industries, which have obtained for the country great renown on account of the excellent taste and skill shown by the workmen. We have already referred to the shawl trade. The real richly embroidered shawl is now seldom manufactured, and in its place woollen goods of cheaper quality, in the shape of square or oblong shawls, plain or embroidered, are produced. Shawls are of two kinds, loom-wove (*binaut*), where the whole pattern is wrought on the loom with an endless series of threads of all colours, and *amlikar*, in which a foundation is laid of a plain or variously coloured fabric, the surface of which is minutely worked over by hand in patterns embroidered in fine woollen thread or silk. In shawl goods the qualities of fineness and softness depend on the wool used. A shawl-loom is worked thus:—The pattern is first drawn on paper, and from the picture a rough sketch is produced. From this the master-workman dictates the pattern, so many red threads, so many blue, and so on. The working weavers follow his dictation, and thus the pattern is evolved. This special training goes on from generation to generation. The shawls are made in small pieces, which are eventually sewn together. The hand-made shawls, which do not touch the loom at all, are similarly made in pieces, which are joined together afterwards. The best kind of woollen fabric is known as *pashmina*. Coarse inferior wool is used in the manufacture of *pattu*, of which various patterns in imitation of English tweeds are now made. A good piece of *pattu* is not a bad imitation of real Scotch home-spun, though, of course, much inferior in finish and durability. Kashmir embroideries are famous for their fineness, elegance of design, and beautiful arrangement of colour. The workmen have some practical knowledge of what the complementary colours are, and know that setting a colour besides its complement sets out both to the greatest effect. Those who are interested in the shawl trade will find a capital description of the same in Moorcroft's " Travels in the Himalayan Provinces," and in Vigne's " Travels in Kashmir, etc." The variety of Kashmir shawls is great ; the best way to become a judge of these, and also of the embroidery on fine *pattu*, is to visit the large shops where articles from a cover for a sofa to the most expensive *pashmina* shawls may be seen in great abundance and variety.

The cotton grown in the valley the people spin themselves, and cotton goods are manufactured without the help of machinery of any sort. Sticks about four feet long are run into the ground in a straight line at equal distances—about two or three feet—apart, according to the length of the cloth to be manufactured. The cotton is then laid alternately in and out of the sticks by women, or men, and boys, walking up and down the entire length, till the threads lie one on top of the other to the required width—usually one yard. The sticks and the cotton are then withdrawn from the earth, and the whole is stretched tight, and dressed with a wet comb-like brush. In this way several yards of cotton cloth are manufactured in a few days. The cost of imported piece-goods is greater than that of cloth manufactured by the above original process. Boat-women are to be found spinning cotton at every spare moment they may have. .. ..

The *papier maché* work of Kashmir was at one time highly esteemed in England, but latterly the demand has fallen off. The designs are traced on *papier maché* or on wood, and the colours employed are, in the best articles, admirably blended. Boxes, card trays, little tea-tables, and a great variety of other articles are made. The work is called *kalamdani*, as pen cases, ornamented by this process, are made in large numbers. A similar style of work is often applied to various larger articles, and sometimes even to the walls and ceilings of rooms. An excellent example of this could at one time have been seen on the ceiling of the Darbar Hall at Srinagar. The colours are usually very well combined, but the inferior work is thick and coarse compared with the best. A very little experience will enable a European to discover the difference between good and bad. ... ...

Silver and gold and copper, enamelled and gilt work is carried on largely in Srinagar. Kashmir enamel is famous all over India, and is highly priced. The metal employed is generally silver alloyed with copper, on which the patterns, consisting of metal dies, are hammered in. The colours used are generally blue and red, and sometimes yellow cups, trays, and bowls are ornamented by this work. The most delicate designs and patterns are used.

Wood-carving is an old industry in Kashmir, and during recent years great impetus has been given to the trade. Carved wooden tables with copper tops, plain or enamelled, are now in great demand. Beautiful ceilings are made by joining together chips of deodar.

Paper is now made in the jail near Hariparbat. It is hand-made and smooth, and strong like parchment.

Leather goods, guns, swords and various metal articles, such as knives and surgical instruments, are also manufactured in Kashmir.

The Kashmiris have always been celebrated for elaborating the decorative details of good designs, whether in metal work, hammered or cut, enamelling, or weaving. The shawls and metal articles of Kashmir are remarkable for the exquisite art lavished on them.

Wine is made at Gopkar on the Dal lake from grapes grown near Chishma Shahi. The prices are as follows:—Claret Rs. 14 per dozen bottles; White Wine Rs. 12 per dozen. Cognac Rs. 3 per bottle, and Brandy No. 1 Rs. 2, and No. 2 Re. 1 per bottle.

Carpets are manufactured in Kashmir. Those who are interested in this branch of industry should visit the extensive factories of Messrs Hadow and Co. and those of M. Duvereigne.

Sericulture was once a very thriving industry, but the silkworms became infected with febrine, and the industry completely died out. Endeavours to resuscitate it have given encouraging results.

The natives are always inclined to be imaginative in the prices they ask, and those who wish to buy Kashmir art work would do well to be guided by others, who know what the price should be.

Silver articles should be bought with caution, as for want of any system of Government assaying alloy is largely used. The usual rate is 2 annas per tola for plain work, 3 annas for the best kind, and 4 annas for gold enamelled work. Copper with gold enamelling is sold at 3 annas per tola or a rupee weight.

The prices of carved walnut-wood tables with copper tray tops vary according to the quality, but Rs. 50 should procure a very handsome one. It would not be quite fair to name any particular dealer in any of the Kashmir manufactures, mainly because those who are leading men one season are apt to be low in the list the next ; and the work is often altered and improved, so it is best to let each visitor choose his own dealer.

BOTANY.

The deodar or Himalayan cedar (cedrus libain var Deodara) is the finest tree in Kashmir. It is found on mountain ranges from 7,000 to 12,000 feet above the sea level. It grows sometimes to a height of from 100 to 200 feet, with a girth of from 20 to 40 feet. The deodar forests in Kashmir are very extensive. The blue pine (pinus excelsia, *kāiru*), yew (taxus baccata, *postil*), elm (ulmus sp. and ulmus wallichiana) are also met with. The ash (fraxinus floribrenda, *hona*) is largely used for making paddles. The plane tree (platanus orientales, *chenar*), probably introduced by the Moguls, grows to a great size, is extremely beautiful, and the noblest tree in the valley. It is met with everywhere and affords ample shade. Poplars (populus nigra and alba safeda) are planted in formal rows or squares. In and near.

Srinagar there are large numbers of these trees, and they attain a great height. The poplar avenue in Srinagar is one of the sights of the city, and the grove of poplars at the entrance of the Gures valley is magnificent. Two kinds of willow are to be seen, and the maple (acer sp., *kamar*), hazel (corylus colurna, *virin*) and hawthorn (cratægus or yacertha, *ring*). Junipers and rhododendrons grow on the mountains at a height of 11,000 feet, whilst in the numerous valleys, roses, wild and cultivated, bloom in profusion. Fruit trees grow wild in all parts of the valley—apple, cherry, pear, quince, pomegranate, apricot, peach, plum, mulberry, walnut, almond and hazelnut. The vine is often found spreading over the branches of these trees, and grapes in the season are abundant. Grafted fruit trees, grown in Srinagar, yield excellent varieties of peaches, pears, apples, cherries, apricots, greengages, and plums. The jargenal pears are very luscious and delicious. The wild strawberry, raspberry, blackberry and currant are also met with. Vegetables are abnudant in Srinagar, and all kinds of English vegetables grow in profusion. On the Dal lake there are floating gardens where large quantities of cucumbers, water-melons, and tomatoes are grown. These are sold very cheaply. Several medicinal plants are found in Kashmir, such as aconite, hyoscyamus, colchicum, belladona, cannalis indica and podophylum, besides many plants used in medicine by the native doctors. The *singhara*, the horned water-nut or water-chestnut (trapa bispenosa) grows in very large quantities on the Dal and the Wular lakes. In the latter the produce is some thousands of tons annually. The trapa bicornis is found in the

Dal: the fruit resembles the head of an ox in miniature. These fruits ripen in October. The *singhara* is the food of a great number of people. The fruit is dried and made into flour. It is very nutritious. The stem of the lotus called *nadur* is eaten fried or cooked with meat, especially in the winter, when other vegetables cannot be had. Mushrooms (agaricus sp.) are common. Rice is the staple food of the Kashmiri. Maize, wheat, barley, millet, buck wheat, tobacco, cotton, amaranth, sesame, poppy, hops, saffron and several kinds of pulse are grown.

Sport in Kashmir.

There is plenty of good shooting to be had in the mountains surrounding the vale of Kashmir, and beyond in the direction of Gilgit, Skardu, Ladak, Wardwan, and Kishtwar.

Bears are found in all parts of the Kashmir State; of the brown or red species there are two varieties, one inhabiting the lower ranges, the other (the *ursus arctus*) higher up the mountains. The black bear is usually found lower down. In "The Sportsman's Guide to Kashmir and Ladak," by Captain Ward, of the Bengal Staff Corps, published in 1882, it is stated that the black bear or *harput* of Kashmir is steadily decreasing in numbers. They are easily shot, and sportsmen usually go after them. The greater number are killed in walnut and apple trees and in maize fields. The fur is best in November. The male is sometimes 6 feet 6 inches in length, but usually under 6 feet; the female is much smaller, and the coat seldom good. In the month of March and as late as the middle of May the skin is valuable, but not afterwards. The black bear is found in the Lolah, Sindh, and Liddar valleys, and other parts of the valley.

The brown or red bear is more difficult to shoot; it has a fine coat from October to the middle of May. The same authority states that the length of this animal averages a little over 6 feet. The places where this animal is found, are chiefly in Gurais and Tilail, reached from the Sindh valley from Kangan, Wangat, and Haramuk; and then in the direction of Dras and Zojila. Wardwan is also recommended by Captain Ward. The routes to these places are given in another page.

Leopards are found in nearly all parts of the Kashmir valley. The ounce or white leopard is said to have been seen in Tilail, but his habitat is defined by Captain Ward to be in the Nubra valley, on the Leh road; or at Sooroo; or the Krishye, a spot in which numerous ibex are found. Skins of the white leopard are sometimes sold in Srinagar at from Rs. 20 to Rs. 30 each.

The *bara singha* or swamp deer is found throughout the Panjal range generally, except where it slopes towards the plains. It is rarely met with before the middle of September, but is occasionally seen in August with fully developed horns; the antlers are perfect in the month of October. The authority already quoted states that this stag is more numerous in the south-east, in the direction of Kishtwar, Badrawar, and Chumba. In the valley, *nullahs* in the Sindh valley should be searched; or Bandipura, on the Wular lake, or towards Dandwar on the Pir Panjal route; the Liddar valley above Eishmaken, and Naobog on the route to Vernag. These places, and especially the Sind valley, are recommended for winter shooting, for they have the advantage of being near Srinagar. Stags are found in the State preserves in the Wangat, at Khunuh near Panpur, and at Tral.

The ibex is found in the northern parts of Kashmir. Wardwan is a good locality, and at Sooroo they are said to abound. These fine animals are also found in every part of Kashmir where there are high and pre-cipitous mountains, especially at Tilail. The length of the horn varies from 45 to 50 and 52 inches. The months of April, May and June are said to be the best' for following ibex. In the two following months the animal ranges far and wide, and can only be got at by tedious and difficult climbing.

The *yural*, or Himalayan chamois, is found in large numbers on the Panjal range, and in Kishtwar.

The *khakar*, or barking deer, is common upon the southern and western slopes of the Pir Panjal range. This beautiful little animal is also often come across in the lower valleys inside the Kashmir basin.

The *markhor*, or serpent-eater, is a species of gigantic goat. It is found all over the Pir Panjal, beyond the Baramulla pass, and upon the mountains between the Jhelum and Kishenganga rivers. Captain Ward, in his "Sportsman's guide," says that this splendid wild goat is more difficult to get than the ibex, and that to shoot one with horns of over 50 inches in length "is worth many long days of really hard work."

The destruction of musk-deer is now prohibited by the Kashmir Darbar. Owing to the valuable musk-pouch in the abdomen of the male, it was very persis-tently sought after by native *shikaris*, and the order was

necessary to prevent its entire extinction. The animal,
called the *kustoorah* or *rous* by the Kashmiris, is found
at various altitudes ranging from 6,000 to 13,000 feet.

The *serrow* or buz-i-kohi. and the *thar*, a species of
mountain goat, are found upon the Panjal range. The
serrow is also found in Kishtwar and in the Sindh and
Liddar valleys. The horns are from 10 to 12 inches.
The *thar* is not common in any part of the valley except
in the Pir Panjal, Kishtwar, and Badrawar. The horns
are usually under 14 inches in length.

Wolves are numerous in the mountains. Foxes, large
and full brushed like the English animal, are plentiful.

The *burhel (ovis nahura)* is found in Ladak. The
horns average 24 inches, and a head of 27 inches is
considered to be very good. Some account of the
habitats of this animal and how it may be shot, and
also regarding the *ovis ammon*, the *ovis vignei*, and the
oorial, will be found in Captain Ward's book. Sportsmen also should not fail to consult the capital volumes
published by General Kinloch on large game shooting.

A species of marmot, called *drum* or *pua*, is found
amongst the rocks at a high elevation ; it is as large as
a fox, of a dull yellowish colour, with tawny belly, the
head, back and tail being marked with a darker stripe,
distinguishable at a considerable distance. The otter
is frequently met with in the rivers ; the porcupine is
found in Kishtwar.

The yak found in Ladak and Thibet is very difficult
to obtain ; the bull's hide with the hair in good condition is considered a better trophy than the horns. The
yak is found beyond Leh chiefly, but the distance from
the valley of Kashmir and the time and trouble in

hunting it are serious obstacles to the greater number of visitors to Kashmir. Besides the yak there are the following animals in Thibet. The antelope, ravine deer, the wild ass, the lynx, wolf and wild dog. Captain Ward has something to say about shooting all these animals. The wild dog is found in Kashmir, in Tilail, in the western, and a few also in the eastern, end of the valley.

Of the game birds in Kashmir, the black *chikor*, and grey and snow species of partridge are met with in many parts. The *chikor (cucabis chikor)* is commonly found in the neighbourhood of Avantipore, and the adjacent hills; also above Pampur, and round the Dal lake near Srinagar, in the Liddar valley, and near Baramulla. The varieties of pheasants are the argus, *manal, kallich, koklas,* and the snow pheasant. The argus is met with in the hills near Thanna Mundi on the Pir Panjal route. Quail, jacksnipe and woodcock are found in Kashmir, but the sport is reported to be very limited.

Waterfowl of all sorts abound in the winter months on the Wular and other lakes. Teal are seen in the Anchar lake, and during midwinter on Manesbal lake. Bald-coots, moorhens, dab-chicks, terns and grebes are constantly to be found in the autumn and winter. The *sarus,* or gigantic crane, is often seen on the marshes, and a small kind of pelican.

Almost every kind of bird known in England is to be found in the valley, blackbirds, wrens, titmice, larks, swallows—which migrate in the winter—thrushes, robins, chaffinches, goldfinches, linnets, etc. Sportsmen should be careful about snakes and poisonous reptiles. Near Sonamarg and **Lar** the poisonous *gaus* is common, and on the hills on the Dal near Nishat Bagh the terrible *puhur* is often met with.

Fishin is a sport that few of the visitors to Kashmir indulge in. Mahseer is the finest fishing, and in the valley near Sopur in the Jhelum is the best place; some very large mahseer have been caught here. On the Pir Panjal route, before coming to the pass, mahseer and trout are caught in some of the rivers met with on those marches. In the valley again another good spot for fishing is just below Sumbal bridge, below Shadipore, and near the canal leading to Manesbal lake. June, July and August are the best months for this locality. The streams near Naobog, at the east end of the valley, contain plenty of fish, but they are not large. There are fish in abundance, but not large, in the Dal lake. For sportsmen January, February and March, if the snow is deep, are the best for stag shooting. For ibex and *markhor* from the middle of April to the middle of June is a sure time. After the middle of June to the middle of September there is very little sport to be had in the lower valleys, both on account of the heat, and because the bigger game has migrated to inaccessible heights. The best time for bear is from the middle of September to the middle of November. In this last month the fur is at its best. This season is also good for *chikor* shooting. In the winter, the lakes swarm with waterfowl, but the birds are very wary and not easy to approach.

GEOLOGY.

The old tradition that at one time the vale of Kashmir was completely occupied by a large lake is confirmed

by the observations of modern geologists. The soil of
the lower plain of Kashmir is loam or clay, the surface
of which has been formed by deposits of river alluvium.
In the lakes now existing lacustrine deposits are still
being made. The *kharewas* or plateaus, to which reference has already been made, are formed of beds of
clay or sand. Drew gives the geological formation
of the *kharewa* at Piru near Islamabad as follows :—

Rather coarse drab or brown sand mixed with pebbles ...	20 feet.
Fine, soft brown sand	3 ··
Hard, very fine grained sand ...	15 ,,
Blue sandy clay	5
Fine soft sand	5
Coarse sand, as in the uppermost stratum	2 ,,

Similar beds lie all through a section of 250 feet.

In some parts of the valley are found hills of pala-
zoic limestone showing phenomena which distinctly
connects them with the old lake. Beds of a conglomerate of rounded pebbles of limestone and sand and
calcareous mud are evident. These pebble beds are
supposed to have been a single beach, formed at the
foot of a limestone cliff which encircled the lake.
Fresh water shells have also been found in the beds.
The flat tops of the *kharewas* are considered to have
formed the original surface of the deposits. Drew con-
siders that the level of the great lake could not have
been much less than 7,000 feet above the sea. Some
strata, consisting of beds of conglomerate, sand, and
loam, with which are mixed many species of land
and fresh water shells, with plants and minute fish
scales, are found in many places between Haripur and

Baramulla. The Panjal mountains are chiefly of igneous origin. The hills on the south, south-eastern, and south-western parts of the valley are composed of grey-coloured compact limestone, containing here and there marine fossils, with belemnites and small shells. Harmukh is composed of granite, but elsewhere this stone is rarely met with. The ranges intervening between Kashmir and the plains are generally of Sienitic rock, slate, schist, sand-stone, and pebbly conglomerate.

As is well known, earthquakes are very common in Kashmir, showing that volcanic action is still at work. An earthquake which took place in 1552 A. D., proved very disastrous. Vigne mentions an earthquake as having taken place on the 26th June, 1828.

The great earthquake on the morning of 30th May, 1885, is one that will long be remembered in the vale of Kashmir. At 3 o'clock on that morning a violent shaking of the houses was felt which lasted for several seconds. In this short time several houses in Srinagar fell, killing some 200 people; the barracks on the maidan near the Amira Kadal came down, burying many soldiers and some 60 cavalry horses. The palace of Sha Gharri was seriously injured, and general consternation prevailed. The area of the shock, as far as the vale of Kashmir was concerned, was from Srinagar to Baramulla, the centre being at the latter place. At the village of Laridura, in the low hills 10 miles south of Baramulla, large landslips occurred; and at Pattan, half-way between Srinagar and Baramulla, an old Buddhist temple in ruins was nearly destroyed. At Sopur, the town was nearly destroyed, and at Baramulla similar destruction was caused. The number of deaths was

officially stated at 3,390, of which 2,700 occurred between Sopur and Baramulla, including the localities already mentioned near the latter place. Besides this
loss of life, more than 6,000 houses and huts were destroyed, and large numbers of sheep and cattle killed,
the lower part of the houses being used by the cattle
at night. The shocks, which commenced on the 30th
May, were followed in the first hour, after the first great
shock, by 6 severe shocks, followed by 19 more, making
25 shocks in 37 hours, and for some days afterwards
they continued at the rate of 3 or 4 every 24 hours.
They gradually became less frequent, but were occasionally severe, and with less frequency took place for
more than twelve months afterwards. In short, the
great earthquake of 30th May, 1885, may certainly be
regarded as one of the most severe shocks ever experienced in Kashmir.

MINERALOGY.

In spite of assertions to the contrary, the mineral resources of Kashmir are great, though they still remain
undeveloped. Iron is found in some parts of the valley,
and at one time the State had smelting works at Shar,
a few miles east of Srinagar near Panpur, and at Sof
near Nobuk in the east end of the valley. Of the two,
the works at Sof were the most important. The
quality of Kashmir iron is said, however, not to be very
good, Mr. Latouche considering the ore poor. Mr. Pres-
tage, of Darjeeling-Himalayan railway fame, visited
Kashmir a few years ago with the view of improving
the iron industry, but so far no steps have been
taken. It is said that veins of copper exist in some

places, and that they were worked in the time of the Pathans. No coal has yet been found, though some of Zanskar rocks resemble this substance. There are several sulphur springs, but native sulphur is scarce.

ARCHÆOLOGY.

There are many ancient buildings in Kashmir. During the time of the Hindu kings before the Muhammadan invasion several temples were erected, monuments were raised, and the sources of springs enclosed and built over. The Muhammadan rulers added further architectural structures, but the slow hand of time or the sudden devastation of an earth-quake have totally destroyed many and injured others. To the historian and antiquarian the buildings still existing are full of interest, and afford many clues to the strange past of the country. A brief account of some of these buildings may be interesting to the general reader.

The Temple of Shankaracharjya, standing on the crest of the Tukht-i-Suleiman, is a very old building. It is built on solid rock, with an octagonal stone founda-tion supporting a square building, and is visible from a great distance. Within the temple there is a Shiva Linga. Two indistinct Arabic inscriptions can still be traced. They were probably put there long after the temple was built. General Cunningham says of this temple: " It is now called Shankracharjya, but the Brahmans in the valley were unanimous in their belief that its original name was Zishteshwara. Its erection they ascribe to Jaloka, the son of Asoka, who reigned about 220 B.C. The style has close affinity to the form

of the common Hindu temples of Bengal." Lieutenant Cole also notices the likeness in style which he
attributes to a common origin. " In Bengal, the pedi-
ments and gables are slightly curved and much more
numerous, but in both Kashmir and Bengal the pri-
mary form was the square block surmounted by a
pyramidal roof. The mode of elaborating the plan remained the same in both countries, and consisted in the
addition of one or more projections to each of the original four sides of the square."

Zainulabdin's Tomb.—During the reign of Sikandar,
who died in 1416 A.D., a large number of Hindu
buildings were desecrated and destroyed. The tombs
of Sikandar's wife and son, Zainulabdin, were built on
the foundations and with the materials of an ancient
Hindu temple. (An interesting temple, which probably
dates from the 5th century, is to be seen in a state of
ruin, at a place between Rampor and Baramulla. It
formerly contained an image of Durga.

Temple of Martand, or the Sun.—This temple, which is
supposed to have been built by Rainaditya (480-555
A.D.), is situated about 3 miles east of Islamabad.
There are three halls in the building, called Ardha-
mandap, Antarula, and Garbha Griha. Of the ruins of
Martand, Vigne says:—" Without being able to boast
either in extent or magnificence of an approach to
equality of the Temple of the Sun at Palmyra or the
ruins of the palace at Persepolis, the Panda Koru
or Martand is not without pretensions to a locality of
scarcely inferior interest, and deserves to be ranked
with them as the leading specimen of a gigantic
style of architecture that has decayed with the religion

it was intended to cherish and the prosperity of a
country which it could not but adorn. In situation it
is far superior to either. Palmyra is surrounded by
an ocean of sand, and Persepolis overlooks a marsh;
but the Temple of the Sun, or Martand, is built on a
natural platform at the foot of some of the noblest
mountains, and beneath its ken lies what is undoubtedly
the finest and most *pronoucée* valley in the known world.
The prospect from the green slope behind is seen to the
greatest advantage upon the approach of evening, when
the whole landscape is yet in sunshine, but about to
undergo a change; when the broad daylight still rests
upon the snowy peaks of the Pir Panjal, but commences
a retreat before their widening shadows in the valley
beneath them. The luminous and yellow spot, in which
we recognise the foliage of the distant chinar tree, is
suddenly extinguished; village after village becomes
wrapt in comparative obscurity, and the last but bril-
liant beams of an Asiatic setting sun repose for a while
upon the grey walls that seem to have been raised on
purpose to receive them, and display the ruins of their
own temple in the boldest and most beautiful relief."

The following temples are supposed to have been
built by the Pandus :—(1) Banyar temple, dedicated to
Bhavani; (2) temples at Pattan; (3) Pandrenthan, near
Srinagar.

Ruins at Avantipur.—These temples were built by
Avantivarma, between 850 and 880 A.D. Lieutenant Cole
conjectures that they were the loftiest buildings in India.

Temples at Rajdhanibal and Nagbal.—There are thirteen
temples in this group of buildings. General Cunningham fixes the date of their erection at 220 B.C.

Besides the buildings enumerated above, there are various other ruins to be found in different parts of the valley. Solitary stone pillars can be seen in several dlaces. During the Muhammadan occupation many Hindu temples were converted into *masjids*.

CHAPTER IV

SRINAGAR AND ITS SURROUNDINGS.

The city of Srinagar, seen from the river Jhelum, which divides it into two portions, has, notwithstanding the dilapidated state of so many of the houses, a pleasing, picturesque, and even, to quote the remark of the author of " The Abode of Snow," " a very fine appearance " It has been compared to Florence. To quote Mr. Wilson again, " as the Kashmiri has been called the Neopolitan of the East, so his capital has been compared to Florence, and his great river to the Arno." The town lies for about two miles on both sides of the Jhelum, which makes a graceful sweep through it, having a breadth of about 88 yards and a depth of about 18 feet, increased by floods in the early part of the season, or during the rains, from 10 to 20 feet more. Sometimes during the summer, owing to sudden thaws of snow on the mountains, or unusually heavy rain, the river will overflow its banks and flood the surrounding country. The Jhelum is the high street of the city. Sir Richard Temple says that " Srinagar is as much a water-city as Venice, or even more so."

Srinagar (or Surjyanagar, " The City of the Sun,") is stated to have been founded in A.D 59. Another statement is that it was founded in the sixth century by Rajah Pravarsane, but it is doubtful whether it was the capital of Kashmir at these early periods. The ruins of another city, which was for some time the capital, are pointed out about five miles east of Srinagar, at Pandritan. Srinagar has, however, been the capital for several centuries. It is situated about midway down the valley in latitude 30° 5′ 31″ north and longitude 54° 51′ east. The two portions of the town are connected by seven bridges over the river. It is built at an elevation of about 5,276 feet above sea level, and is surrounded by low swampy tracts. There are nearly 22,500 houses in the city, which contains a population of about 118,960. The town may be said to lie at the feet of two hills, Harri Parbat, about 500 feet high, and Tukht-i-Suleiman, 1,000 feet high. On the top of Harri Parbat is a fort, built by the Emperor Akbar to overawe the inhabitants who once showed symptoms of rebellion. The fort consists of two squares, in one of which stands a Hindu temple. The fort is said to have consisted originally of nothing but strong outer walls, the buildings within being attributed to Ata Muhammad Khan in the reign of Zaman Shah Durani. A tower within is called after Shah Shuja-ul-Mulk, who was at one time imprisoned there. An armoury is to be seen, in which there are a few brass guns. The ex-Rajah of Hunza now lives in a room within the fort as a State prisoner. On the Kati Darwaza, the principal gateway, is a Persian inscription stating that the stone wall surrounding the fort was built by the Emperor Akbar in A.D. 1590, at a cost of one crore of rupees. The wall is three miles long, 28 feet high and 13 feet thick, the bastions, placed at intervals of 50 yards, are 34 feet high, and loop-holed. From the excellent view of Srinagar from the top of this hill, the peculiar characteristics of the city may be easily noticed. On the southern side of the hill is the ziarut of Makdum Sahib, to which the Muhammadans approach with great sanctity.

The other hill, Tukht-i-Suleiman, 6,263 feet above sea level, is far more interesting than Harri Parbat. From the summit—which is reached by a good path, though a little steep in some places, from the village of Drogjun at the foot, behind the Munshi Bagh—an extended view of the windings of the Jhelum and the country beyond is obtained, as well as of the city of Srinagar, the city canals, poplar avenue, the Dal lake, and all the surrounding hills. The peculiar curves in the river Jhelum immediately below this hill are said to have given the design for the shawl pattern which is still adhered to as tenaciously as ever.

The building on the Tukht-i-Suleiman may be the remains of a Buddhist temple, of which the other ruins on the sides of the hill may have been part, but the present temple is not considered typical of the Kashmiri style of architecture. Its origin has been put as far back as 200 B.C., when Asoka introduced Buddhism into Kashmir. It is built in an octagonal form, of solid masses of stone, some of them very large, and is approached from the east by stone steps. After passing through an archway, there is a flight of limestone steps which lead to the temple, which is circular inside, 14 feet diameter, 11 feet high, with flat roof. Four pillars support the roof; on the floor is a quadrangular platform on which is a *lingam*, with a serpent coiled round it. On one of the pillars are Persian inscriptions; one states that the *lingam* was placed there by a *sonar*, a goldsmith, named Raji Hashti, in the year 54 of the Hindu era, about 1876 years ago ; on the same pillar near the pavement another inscription, the date of which is not visible, states " He who raised this idol was Kwajah Rokm, son of Mirjan." A few years ago the *lingam* was one day discovered broken. It has since been replaced by a new one. The more correct account of this temple is probably the following from " Fergusson's Architecture in the Himalayas." He writes regarding this " anomalous building " :—

" The temple itself is far from having an ancient look. The one most like it that I am acquainted with, is that erected by Cheyt Sing at Ramnuggar, near Benares, at the end of the last century. I know of no straight-lined pyramid of a much older date than that, and no temple with a polygonal plan combined with a circular cell, as is the case here, that is of ancient date. The four pillars in the cell, with the Persian inscriptions upon them, are avowedly of the seventeenth century. It is suggested, however, that they belong to a repair: my conviction is, from a review of the whole evidence, that the temple, as it now stands, was commenced by some nameless Hindus in honour of Siva during the tolerant reign of Jehangir, and that the building was stopped at the date engraved on the staircase A. H. 1069 (A. D. 1659), the first year of the reign of the bigot Aurungzebe. It was unfinished, and has consequently remained a ruin ever since, which may give it an ancient look, but not such as to justify any one putting it 1,879 years before what seems to be its true date, as is done by General Cunningham and his follower Lieutenant Cole " Mr. Fergusson also says that the small temples alongside are of the same date as this one.

On the right bank of the river near the Munshi Bagh are several nicely-built buildings, occupied by European officials in State employ. There is a barrack here in which quarters are sometimes available for married visitors. Within the Munshi Bagh is a camping ground and the recently-built church. Below this is the new canal with a lock gate, leading to the Dal. A boat will carry a visitor from the Bagh to the lake by way of this canal. Near by is the Kashmir Subscription Library, which has a large stock of books and English and Indian newspapers. It is open to all who care to pay the moderate subscription. The visitor will next notice the Residency, the approach to which from the river is by a marble flight of steps; close by, covered with trees, is an island on which lives a solitary *fakir*. Visitors sometimes pitch their tents here, but it should be remembered that during the rains the island is liable to be covered with water. A little further down are the bungalows occupied by the Residency vakil and clerks and the Post Office. Near by is the office of Messrs. Dhanjibhoy and Son. Behind these houses lies the polo ground, at one end of which is the Residency surgeon's bungalow. At the back of the polo ground, between it and the Chinar Bagh, is the Samandar Bagh, in which stand the houses occupied by the Assistant Resident, Settlement Commissioner, Gilgit, the Transport Officer, and others, as well as the Roman Catholic Chapel. Below the Kotni Bagh (Residency) is the Hari Singh Bagh, which was formerly used as a camping ground for bachelors. The Imperial Telegraph Office stands here. A little further on are the shops for the sale of English goods and the office of the Punjab

G

Banking Corporation, Limited. Further down the river
is the Shekh Bagh, in which is the little cemetery. The
house in the centre was originally a mosque. It was
for a time used as a Residency, and later on was
occupied by the chaplain, the upper story being used as
a church. At present the Shekh Bagh contains two
houses occupied by missionaries. Below the Shekh
Bagh is the Chief Court. On the opposite side of the
river is the Lalmandi Palace, so-called because of the
colour predominating, in which is located the Meteorological Observatory. The Maharajah rarely makes use
of the palace, which is reserved for distinguished
guests and State banquets. Near by are the imposing
buildings of the State Hospital. This hospital accommo-
dates 100 in-patients and gives gratuitous medical
relief to about 250 people daily. A new wing has recently been added as a memorial to the late Maharajah
Ranbir Singh. Behind the buildings is the maidan
used as a parade ground for the troops in the cantonment close by. Passing round the bend of the river,
the first of the seven bridges, called the Amira . Kadal,
is seen. The bridge is of solid construction, and was
built quite recently, near the old Amira Kadal, which
has been demolished, as it was considered unsafe for
wheeled traffic. Below the first bridge on the left
bank of the river is the Shergarhi—a rectangular enclosure 400 by 200 yards. It is surrounded by double,
loopholed, stone walls connected by numerous bastions
on its three land sides. On the fourth side, facing the
river, are a row of high-walled buildings of quaint
architecture. Inside the Shergarhi is a bazar, many
houses, offices, storehouses, treasury, and the Royal

Palace with the gilt temple. The new palace, which is fast coming to a completion, is of modern design, but attached to it are several old buildings. At the top of the steps near the Royal Temple is kept the Visitors' Book, in which callers at the palace sign their names. The door leads to a courtyard, in the centre of which is a recently-made pavilion, surrounded by houses, one of which is the Durbar Hall, or Golghur. The walls and ceilings of the Golghur are decorated with the most gorgeous colours.

At the junction with the Jhelum of the Sonti-kol, or apple tree canal, is a. temple. The canal leads to the Dal or City lake, passing the Chinar Bagh on the right. On entering the Sonti-kol, a boat has to pass through the recently-constructed lock. A short distance up the canal is the old stone bridge, called the Goa Kadal. A few yards further on at a bend in the canal may be seen several of the Maharajah's boats, moored to the bank. Here are the State workshops. Another bend to the right reveals the Chinar Bagh, and here the view is extremely pretty. To quote the author of "The Abode of Snow," it " presents one of the finest combinations of wood and water in the world " The Chinars are referred to as " mountains of trees, and yet beautiful in shape and colour, with their vast masses of· foliage reflected in the calm, clear water." Just beyond is a fine row of poplar trees, and then another bend in the canal takes the visitor to the gate of the Dal lake, or *Dal-ke-darwaza*. This is a favourite place for bathing and fishing. The canal from Munshi Bagh also joins the lake here. The gates are only open when the water is flowing out of the lake. As soon as the Jhelum is in flood the mass of water stops the outward flow, and the current of the stream being reversed, the doors close of their own accord, and the water is prevented from flowing into the lake; a needful arrangement, for otherwise the overflow that would ensue would flood the portions of the city on the canals near the Dal.

DAL OR CITY LAKE.

The gate into the Dal lake is cut through the long high causeway, an old structure thrown up by the Muhammadans, and repaired and heihhtened by the Maharajah. The object is to keep the waters of the Jhelum under restraint during the floods. Next the gate is the village of Drogjun, near a rocky mound, with a tomb on the top; nearer the mountains, on higher ground, stands the Mission Hospital. This hospital is the means of doing great good amongst the Kashmiris. Funds are always required to meet the constant demand for medicines, and visitors would be doing an act of real benevolence by contributing to this hospital.

The Dal lake is a sheet of water about five miles long and 2½ broad, the water is sometimes quite shallow, the deeper parts are not more than 8 or 9 feet, but nearly opposite the Nasim Bagh there is a small spot where the water is about 30 or 40 feet deep. The appearance of the Dal lake is injured by the large overgrowth of rush grass which covers a very large portion of the lake, and before the end of the season is four or five feet above the water : in the centre it is cut down and used in making *chatais*, which are used either as mats or for roofs of houses and covering for

the boats. But the scenery on the lake is very beautiful. The background of mountains, running round
the lake, with distant views of the snowy ranges, the
numerous gorges running far into the mountains, and
down which the water pours into the lovely valleys and
gardens beneath, preserving their beauty and freshness
throughout the year, combine to make as charming a
scene as the fondest lover of Nature could desire to
look upon. Mr. Lawrence says: " Perhaps in the whole
world there is no corner so pleasant as the Dal lake."

The visitor will obtain the best view on the lake by
ordering his boat to be taken up the water in a straight
line from the gate, avoiding a similar channel on the
left. After going for nearly a mile—the hill of Tukht-
i-Suleiman towering on the right the whole way,—a
broad expanse of water is entered, and the view includes the gorge in the far distance in which is the
Chushma Shahi, a beautiful spring of water ; at the spot
where it emerges from the side of the mountain the
Maharajah has erected a summer-house, a square white
building, which catches the eye as soon as this wider
expanse in the lake is reached. At the corner, immediately before entering this expanse, is a spot of clear
water, called Gagribal, where formerly the most costly
Kashmir shawls were brought to be washed. Here too
a spring of water, which the boatmen declare has mar-
vellons qualities, bubbles up. Leaving this corner the
first view on the right is of one of the spurs of the
Tukht-i-Suleiman, near the top of which is the tomb of a
Muhammadan, who left behind him a great reputation
by spending profusely a lakh or two of rupees in enter-
taining the people of Srinagar with *nautches* and continual

easting on the lake. When his fortune was nearly exhansted, he passed away amidst the regrets of those whom he had munificently entertained, and was buried at this spot. He is reported to have spent a great deal more than two lakhs, but as the event occurred about a century ago, the current reports of his great wealth are doubtless exaggerated.

The next obJect is a grove of fine plane trees—a pleasant camping ground. Beyond is a village where are located the buildings connected with the manufacture of wine, now in charge of an Italian gentleman, who will gladly show visitors the distillery and the huge vats in which the wine is stored. Next is a spot known as the Four Chinars. It was once a camping ground, but is now private property. A little beyond a spur of the Tebanwan mountain are the ruins of a large building called Peri Mahall, or the Fairies' Palace, which is said to have been intended for a college, and was built by Prince Dara Shikoh for his tutor, Mulla Shah. The situation commands a fine view of the Dal lake. There is a path to it up the side of the spur. The building is in terraces, on the façades of which are rooms and niches. The intention in putting it there is not clear, but one report states that it was intended for astronomical purposes, particularly for observing the moon. It is also said that some Muhammadans of the *Sufi* sect, of rather infidel tendencies, had special objects of their own in placing the building in the isolated spot it occupies, a spot which must have been even more solitary when it was first built.

The visitor should direct his attention to the floating gardens here, which cover a large space. They are

found also in other parts of this lake   They are prepared at the close or in the spring of the year by cutting the rushes as near the roots as possible at low
water, so that a body of rushes, sometimes 30 or 40
yards long and two or three feet wide, will rise to the
surface, a fairly-solid mass, without roots. The tops
of the rushes are then cut off as low as possible, leaving a
bed on which earth is placed. This long bed is then
towed to a clear part of the lake, and then fixed by
long poles run through it into the mud. On it a
mossy weed, taken from the lake, is formed into clumps
placed at equal distances. On these clumps cucumbers,
tomatoes and such vegetables are grown in large quantities. Little passages running between these gardens
form lines of communication for the owners' boats.
Gardens similar to these may be seen in China.

Passing slowly across this fine piece of water,
the beautiful lotus-leaves and a variety of other
water plants are sure to attract attention, and when
the lovely lotus flowers in July, its beautiful pink and
white leaves expanded to their full size in the sun, form
a really splendid sight. But they are not so strikingly
charming as on the little lake at Manesbal, a description of which will be found further on. A little beyond is Chusma Shahi, a prominent white object at
once seen on entering the wider part of the lake.
There is a path about two miles long from the shore to
the spring. It divides the pieces of ground on which are
grown in terraces the vines from which wine is made
in the buildings already noticed. These vines were imported in cuttings from France some years ago—and
sUcceeded fairly well till a few years ago when the

Phylloxera appeared. The present produce is very poor. Several of the trees on the shore here are over-grown with vines which have for many years been climbing among their boughs, as their thick stems prove. Near here is a mountain spur running down almost to the water's-edge, beside which is a very pretty village called Bren, embedded amongst the trees, a peaceful looking spot. Here at one time lived a pious Mussulman, who planted two plane trees high up the mountain side. It was near these trees that he passed his time in prayer and meditation; beneath them he was buried; they are his tombstone and a lasting memorial of his piety. Just beyond is the Nishat Bagh with a good pleasure-house, kept in repair by the Maharajah, who reserves the house and gardens for his own use. The gardens were laid out by the Emperor Jehangir. The house and pavilions were also built by the same Emperor. This garden is arranged in terraces, the mode always adopted by the Muhammadans, with a stream of water and numerous fountains running through the centre. The water-channel is lined with limestone, and the water is derived from a mountain stream, which runs from a long distance at the foot of the mountains, supplying the other pleasure gardens with water. By the arrangement of these gardens in terraces, water-falls are easily made, and they are very effective. The final water-fall at Nishat Bagh into the lake is over a mass of masonry 20 feet high. The water runs through the garden for irrigation purposes, but when permission is granted for a picnic or pleasure party, the water is turned into the limestone channels, the fountains play, and when the garden is lighted up in the evening, the effect is extremely pretty. A most enjoyable ride can be obtained over a nice road from Munshi Bagh to Gupkar distillery and thence to Chima Shahi and further on to Nishat Bagh through the village of Bren. The new Visitors' Cottage Hospital is on the road behind the Munshi Bagh.

A short distance from the Nishat Bagh is the Sona Lanka, or Golden island, nearly opposite the village of Bren. The beauty of the garden has long since departed, and it is only interesting because of its connection with Jehangir and his beautiful and accomplished wife, Nur Jahan, to whom is probably due the credit for having selected the lovely spots throughout the Happy Valley where the Emperor's pleasure gardens are to be found. The next spot to visit is the Shalimar garden (abode of the Goddess of Love), which resembles on a smaller scale the garden at Lahore of the same name. It is approached by a long canal, but owing to the difficulty of getting a boat near the garden entrance, the visitor has often to walk a longish distance over an unattractive road. It is reported that it was in this garden that the Emperor Jehangir enjoyed the intense delight of making up the quarrel he had with "his Nur Mahal, his Harem's Light." The poet Moore has immortalised the scene, which he closes thus :—

> And well do vanished frowns enhance
> The charms of every brightened glance ;
> And dearer seems each dawning smile
> For having lost its light awhile ;
> And happier now for all her sighs,
> As on his arm her head reposes
> She whispers him with laughing eyes,
> " Remember, love, the feast of roses."

The garden is laid out in four terraces with a tank
or reservoir in the middle   The further end of the
garden was given up to the Imperial ladies ; here   there
is a very handsome pavilion of black marble, beautifully
carved, standing in the centre of a square reservoir
lined with marble.   The garden is nearly 600 feet long
and more than 250 wide.   There are some very fine plane
trees.   Picnic parties here are very enjoyable, and the
return to Srinagar in the bright moonlight is a delightful finish to a long day of pleasure.

> "Oh ! to see it at sunset when warm o'er the lake
> Its splendour at parting a summer eve throws,
> Like a bride full of blushes when lingering to take
> A last look at her mirror at night ere she goes."--
>   *Moore.*

Leaving Shalimar the lake is crossed to Nasim Bagh,
or the Tepher Garden.   This place is called Ragunath-
pur.

On the way not far from the shore are some buildings
erected for the purpose of manufacturing silk.   The
Nasim is one of the most delightful spots on the Dal.
It was constructed by Akbar with a revetment wall, stairs
and terraces.   There are avenues of chinars, and the
view of the Dal with the circling wall of mountains reflected in it is exquisite.   Near here the rivulet, called
Telbal, enters the lake.   It is a famous place of resort
of the Kashmiris, rich and poor alike, who come here
for their picnics and on festive occasions ; the shawl
weavers come here daily.   The water of the Telbal is
remarkable for being very pure and very cold.   The
Telbal rises in the mountain behind Shalimar Bagh.
Close by is the *Char Chenar* island, called also *Rupa*

Lank or Silver island.   In its early days this island was
doubtless a lovely spot, and enhanced the beauty of
the view from Nasim Bagh ; it is in a sadly neglected
condition now.   At one time a plane tree stood at each
corner, and a stone platform was placed in the centre;
the sides of the island were protected by masonry.
The water is very deep near the Nasim Bagh.   This
garden is now only a large grove of plane trees, some
of them very fine, but several hollow with age, a de-
fect which spoils so many of the plane trees in Kashmir.   Tents may be pitched in this garden ; the view
is remarkably pretty from the shore, but the distance
from Srinagar is just far enough to be inconvenient :
visitors therefore usually camp here for only a few
days.

Proceeding a short distance further, the visitor arrives
at Hazratbal, where there is a celebrated *ziarat*, in
which is preserved in a conical glass phial with a silver
top a hair from the beard of the Prophet Mahommed.
A flight of steps leads up to the *ziarat*.   Festivals are
held here during the year ; in the months of May and
August the hair in the phial is shown, and great
numbers of devout Muhammadans assembles from all
parts of the valley.   From Nasim Bagh the boat may
be taken to Nagin Bagh and to the *nullah* which passes
through Rainawari.   The State Leper Asylum and the
Kashmir Jail may be visited.   At Hassanabad, which
is next reached, is a ruined mosque, once a handsome
building, as the carved limestone remains amply testify.
It is said to have been built by the *Shia* sect of Muhammadans in the reign of Akbar.   The style is the
same as that of the *Patthar masjid*, on the left bank of the

Jhelum, just below the third bridge.   Hindu animosity destroyed this fine mosque when Mean Singh was Governor of Kashmir.   He ordered its destruction, and carried away some of the limestone blocks to form the ghât, at Basant Bagh, opposite the Maharajah's palace.

In this way the most handsome ghât on the banks of the Jhelum was erected.   There is a cemetery adjoining and a wooden mosque built by the *Sunnis* a few years ago.

Further on is a three-arched stone bridge, called Naiwidyar.   On each side of the middle arch is an inscription in Persian.   This bridge marks the commencement of the causeway, four miles long, which runs right across the Dal lake, terminating near the Nishat Bagh.   Finally, the circuit of the lake is completed at the large village of Kraliyar, where there are some old and dilapidated ghâts.

Having seen the Dal lake, the visitor will probably wish to see more of the city of Srinagar than he could from his boat on arrival.   Instead, therefore, of going up the canal opposite the *Sher Garhi*, the boat goes straight on.   To the left runs the Kutikul canal, which passes round the western side of the city and falls into the Jhelum again just below the sixth bridge, called the Naya Kadal   The Kutikul runs between the palaces and Raja Sir Amar Singh's summer house which is a beautiful little villa with an artistically planned garden.   Two Hindu temples and Sirdar Rup Sing's house, are conspicuous objects at this part of the river, and then is reached the second bridge, called the Habba Kadal.   A disastrous fire, which occurred here in 1892, burnt down over 1,500 houses.   After the fire a wide road was

constructed through this part of the city. Just below is
another very large Hindu temple, called the Ragunath
Mandir. Further on is the third bridge, called Fatih
Radal. On each side the river will be seen several good
native shops and residences; a number of manufactures
may be purchased here. Shawls are manufactured at
one or two places on either side the river. The proprietors are always ready to receive visitors and show
them both the loom and the hand work. A visit should
be made to one of these buildings; it is not only interesting to witness the manufacture of these beautiful
fabrics, but it is highly instructive to notice the work-
people, the sort of places in which they work, and the
condition of the streets and surroundings where they
pass the whole of their lives. On the right bank of the
river is a famous mosque called Shah Hamadan. It is
built of cedar, and is very elaborately carved; there is a
golden ball on the top; this finial is used on all the
mosques in Kashmir. It is described as being " a remini-
scence of a Buddhist Tee, very much altered, but still
not so very unlike some found in Nepal." The mode
in which the logs are disposed and ornamented, resembles the ornamentation of the Orissan temples. It has
been considered by competent authority that the roof of
this mosque is probably very similar to that which once
covered the temple at Martand. There is a Persian
inscription inside extolling the virtues of Hamadan and
calling on the faithful to follow his example, " whence
all temporal and spiritual good can be obtained." The
following story connected with Shah Hamadan is believed by the Muhammadans, and is given by Vigne in
his " Travels."—" Timur Lang was one night wandering

in disguise about a street of his capital (Samarkand)
and overheard an old man and his wife talking about
their near prospect of starvation, upon which he
took off an armlet, threw it to them, and departed un-
seen. A pretended *sayyid*, or descendant of the Prophet,
asked them how they came by the armlet, and accused
them of having stolen it. The matter was made known
to Timur, who very sagaciously decreed that the owner
must be the person who could produce the fellow armlet. He then displayed it in his own possession and
ordered the accuser to undergo the ordeal of hot iron.
The latter refused, and was put to death in consequence.
Timur, moreover, put to death all the pretended *say-
yids* in the country. One man, named Sayyid Ali or
Shah-i-Hamadan, who really was a descendant of the
Prophet, accused Timur of impiety, told him that he
(the *sayyid*) would not remain in the country, and by
virtue of his sanctity was able to transport himself
through the air to Kashmir. He descended at the spot
where the mosque now stands, and told the Hindu *fakir*
to depart. The latter refused, upon which Shah-i-Hamadan said he would believe in his sanctity if he could
bring news from Heaven. The *fakir*, who had the care
of numerous idols, immediately despatched one of them
skywards. The *sayyid* with great presence of mind
immediately kicked his slipper after the messenger and
hit it with such force that it fell to the ground. He
then asked the *fakir* how he came to have the power of
making inanimate things move. The latter said it was
due to his charitable actions. Upon this Shah-i-Hamadan thought him worthy of being made a convert
to Islam. In a few days there were so many more

converts that two-and-a-half *kharwars* of Jinyus, or sacred Brahminical threads, were delivered up by Hindu proselytes. The converted *fakir* took the name of Shekh Baba Wali, and a penance of 40 days performed at his shrine is considered the *ne plus ultra* of the meritorious."

Opposite this mosque, on the other side of the river, is a very fine ruin in limestone of a noble mosque, called the Pathar *masjid*, built by Nur Mahal. It is now used as a State granary for rice. Inside, the original design of the building may be seen, not much of it being destroyed. The impression produced on looking at this grand old ruin is similar to that produced on seeing the ruins of some fine old abbey in England. The purpose to which it is now put is to be regretted.

Below the fourth bridge, the Jaina Kadal, is a very old and interesting building called Badshah. It is the tomb of Kashmir's greatest ruler, Zein-ul-ub-din, who was the patron of art and literature, and who introduced the manufacture of shawls.

He succeeded, in A.D. 1416, his father, Sikander, who was nicknamed Butshikan, or idol breaker. The architecture of the enclosure round this tomb has led to some discussion among the learned, but from the experienced judgment of Fergusson it may safely be stated that it was built at the same time as the tomb; others think that it belonged originally to an ancient Kashmiri temple. This enclosure consists of a series of smal pointed arches in rectangular frames such as are frequently found in Muhammadan art, and the peculiarities of the gateways and other parts are such as are found in all contemporary Moslem art in India. The

Moslems in India frequently borrowed details from
the Jains. The niches in the gateways are like those
at Martand and other places ; but, like those at Ahmeda-
bad, are without images, and the arch in brick is radia-
ting, and is certainly not a Hindu arch. The Moslems
copied the Hindus, putting foliage in place of images ;
and doubtless this enclosure was built at the same time
as the tomb it surrounds.

Not far from this tomb, but to be reached only by
passing through some streets in the town, is a very
fine and peculiarly constructed building, the Jumma
masjid. It is, perhaps, owing to its position that it
has been so frequently overlooked, but it is well worthy
of a visit, and of the attention of an artist. It is the
principal mosque in Srinagar, of wooden architecture—
a style which is regarded as an indication of decadence
and decreptitude. The building is constructed on the
usual plan, a courtyard surrounded by cloisters longer
and loftier on the side towards Mecca. The pillars are
of deodar. Inside, the roof of the mosque is very lofty,
and is supported by deodar pillars at least a hundred
feet high, each from a single tree, handsomely carved.
There are many deodar trees in the forests of Kashmir of this great height. The mosque was built by
the Emperor Shah Jehan. In the neighbourhood are
several tombs of some of the ruling families of the
Chaks, who at one time obtained the upper hand in
Kashmir, till they were succeeded by others. It may
be remarked here that similar tombs and masses of
masonry in ruins may be discovered here and there
amidst the wrecks of buildings and the squalid dwelling-
houses of the inhabitants. In the same neighbourhood

is a rude building which, at one time, was used as a mint. The present mint is located at Jamma.

The next place to be noticed is the Maharajgunj, a very imposing looking range of buildings, approached by a long wide flight of steps. At the top is the entrance, up a short narrow street, to the Maharajgunj bazaar, a large square, with shops of the various silver, *papier maché*, and other trades. Many of the specimens of Kashmir work in this bazaar are worth seeing; but the great drawback is, that visitors are so beset by the native tradesmen who, in very broken English, solicit a visit to their shops, that there is little inclination to make more than one or two visits. Here also are located the State School and Dispensary. There are some old buildings hereabouts which might be visited; one of them is the Bulbul Lankor, a mosque of wood, said to be as old as the 12th century, which would make it one of the oldest mosques in the country.

Below the sixth bridge, on the right, is a fine private residence, formerly occupied by the late Pandit Rajkak, who was an influential man among the Kashmiris, and who died in 1865. There is a Hindu temple on the river side of the large garden in front.

Before arriving at the seventh and last bridge, called the Suffa Kadal, there is a fine maidan, called the Idgah, on the right, used as a place of assembly by the Muhammadans. At the northern end is a wooden mosque erected in A.D. 1471. There are some handsome plane and other trees on this maidan, and being backed by the mountains, the view is very pretty. On the opposite side of the water is a serai, built in the form of a square, where traders from Yarkand and Central

H

Asia put the horses they import, themselves, and their goods. A good Yarkand horse may occasionally be met with here. The Suffa Kadal was built by Saif Khan in A.D. 1664. Below this bridge is the *Guzar* or Octroi post, near which is the place of execution. In Kashmir capital punishment take place in the open, and thousands of people assemble on such occasions.

CHAPTER V.

THE EASTERN PORTION OF KASHMIR

FROM SRINAGAR UP THE RIVER JHELUM.

HAVING seen the city of Srinagar and its surroundings, the visitor may prepare for a trip up the
river to Islamabad, or rather to Khanbal, a mile from
that place on the right bank. On the way there he may
visit Pandritan and Pampor, marching from the latter
place to the sulphur and iron springs at Weean (three
miles inland) and visiting two or three adjacent places ;
thence again up the river to Avantipore, where there are
the ruins of a Hindu temple, and then to Khanbal.
Here the boats may be left till the marches to Bawan,
Martand and other places in the neighbourhood have
been made. Afterwards Achibal, Naobog, and Vernag—
the latter the source of the Jhelum—may be visited. The
time occupied in travel will be very pleasantly spent. The
ruins of the Hindu temples are interesting, and the
scenery, particularly about Achibal and Vernag, extremely pretty.

Starting then from the Munshi Bagh in the early
morning, the boats may be sent on to make the long
tedious passage of two or three hours round the curves
in the river to Pandritan ; the march on the road, only
three miles, will be found a pleasant morning's walk.

It is said that at one time the capital of Kashmir
was near Pandritan. Passing on, in hollow ground,
amongst trees and surrounded with water, will be seen
a very excellent example of Kashmiri architecture. The

temples, of which there are ruins at Pandritan, Avantipore, and Martand, are all small, and are copies of their
larger prototype, the ruins of which may be seen in
the Gandhara monasteries near Peshawar. In the usual
style of architecture of these miniature temples there
are four roofs, but in the built examples there have been
found hitherto only two or three, doubtless copied from
the usual wooden roofs common in Kashmir, where the
upper pyramid covers the central part of the building,
and the lower, a verandah, separated from the centre
either by walls or merely by a range of pillars. In the
stone buildings the interval between the two roofs, which
is open in the wooden, is closed. All these roofs are relieved by dormer windows, that is, windows pierced
through the sloping roof; the same steep, sloping lines
are used also to cover the doorways and porches, these
being virtually a section of the main roof itself,
and evidently a copy of the same wooden construction.
The pillars which support the porticos are the most
striking peculiarity of the Kashmiri style, their shafts
being almost identical with those of the Grecian Do-
ric, and unlike anything of the same class found in
other parts of India. Generally they are only three or
four diameters in height, tapering slightly towards the
capital, and adorned with sixteen flutes rather shallower
than those of the Grecian order. Nowhere in Kashmir
are traces found of the bracket capital of the Hindus, nor
of the changes from square to octagon, or to the poly-
gon of sixteen sides, and so on. There can be no
doubt that these *quasi*-Grecian forms were derived from
the monasteries at Gandhara before referred to. The
trefoiled arch, which is everywhere prevalent in Kash-

mir, is a peculiarity not easy to account for, but it was, perhaps, derived from the façades of the *Chaitya* halls of the Buddhists, some examples of which may be seen in the caves at Ajunta. As everywhere in India, architectural decoration is made up of small models of large buildings, applied as decorative features, whenever required. It is thought probable that the trefoiled façade may have been adopted in Kashmir as currently as the simple horse-shoe form was throughout the Buddhist buildings of India. All these features, however, mark a local style differing from anything else in India, pointing certainly to another race and another religion, which cannot at present be traced to their source.

These are the most authoritative opinions yet published on Kashmiri architecture, and the description here given will be found to correspond with the appearance of the ruins at Pandritan and elsewhere in Kashmir. The temple at Pandritan still stands in water, as it always has stood. In the end of the month of June, before the rains, the water is sometimes so low that it is not difficult to walk over the mud and take a look at the interior, especially the roof, which is most distinctly classical, and is ornamented in a way to command admiration. There was originally perhaps a third roof, but that has fallen ; the lower part of the building exhibits all the characteristic features of the Kashmiri style in as much perfection as any other example.

Near this ruin may be seen the lower part of a colossal figure, and a huge *lingam*. During the time the visitor has been looking at the ruins and getting some idea, perhaps for the first time, of Kashmiri architecture, his boats will have reached the shore at Pandritan,

and he may then proceed a short distance further, to
Pundu Chakh, where are the remains of a stone bridge,
thrown across by the Moguls, one of the many substan-
tial evidences of the benefit conferred on the country
by their rule. This bridge is said to have been built
by order of the Emperor Jehangir.

After a few more hours by boat, Pampor is
reached. The distance by road from Srinagar is only
eight miles, but by water it is much longer. There is a
wooden bridge across the river here resembling those at
Srinagar. A fine mosque and a *ziarat* are to be seen
in the town. At the landing place is a grove of plane
trees—a fine spot for a camp. The house on the banks
of the river is reserved for the use of the Maharajah.
From Pampor a visit may be made to Weean—a
pleasant march of three miles towards the mountains.
A few days may be agreeably spent here. Strong sulphurous springs flow from beneath the mountain, the
water being collected in a tank in which are a number
of fish. Being strongly impregnated with iron, the water
has many excellent medicinal qualities. The source of
these springs is called Phak Nag. There is a spring
of fresh water close by called Katish Nag. The adjoining mountains are very different in appearance from
those in other parts of the valley.

Here, and for some distance in an easterly direction,
pyrites abound in the rocks in the hill sides, a combin-
ation of sulphur with iron, copper, and other metals.
From Weean a day's excursion may be made to
Khrew, a very small village, where there is an old relic
of snake-worship in a ruin standing in water. The
building inside is circular, for the convenience of the

huge serpent, which popular superstition still believes
to inhabit the mountain close by. There are here, as
in many other places in the neighbourhood, stones that
have evidently formed part of some temple, with
figures carved on them ; they have been placed in this
and similar spots, sometimes under a tree, by the
Hindus centuries ago, and have been worshipped ever
since. At Shar, a village close by, there are some Státe
iron-works. Iron-works also exist at Sof, not very far
from Achibal, but on a much larger scale

· Returning to Pampor, the saffron gardens should be
looked at. The plant is in appearance exactly like the
common crocus, is also perennial, is cultivated in little
square beds, flowers in October, and from the stigma,
the top of the pistil, is taken the yellow matter, which
forms the saffron. The botanical name of this plant is
Crocus sativus. It is found nowhere else in Kashmir.

At Ladoo, a few miles from Pampor, there is another
ruined temple, similar to that at Pandritan, and at
Payech, on the opposite side of the river, six miles from
Karbarpore, rather more than half way between Pampor and Avantipore, is the ruin of one of the smallest,
but most excellent examples of this style of architecture. Its dimensions are only 8 feet square for the
superstructure and 21 feet high including the basement ;
but with these dimensions it acquires a certain dignity
from being erected with only six stones, four for the
walls and two for the roof. It stands by itself on a
knoll, without any court or other surroundings, and
being dedicated wholly to the gods of the Hindu Pan-
theon, it certainly belongs to an age when their worship had superseded the older faiths of the valley. So

far as is at present known, it belongs to the 13th century, but is probably of a more modern rather than of
a more ancient date. Some writers have fixed an early
age for parts of these old ruins, going as far back as
Asoka, B.C. 250. But though it is known that this
monarch sent missionaries to convert the inhabitants of
Kashmir to the Buddhist faith, and that in the first
century Kanishka, a Buddhist king, was an absolute
monarch in the valley, and, moreover, Hiouen Thsang,
the celebrated Chinese traveller, stayed for two years
in Kashmir, A.D. 633 and 634, to study the forms and
writings of the Buddhists, whose creed he found one of
the dominant faiths of the people, still not a vestige is
to be found of a *chaitya* or a *vihara*; there are mounds
which may contain stupas; but it is considered to be
improbable that they will contain any architectural
forms which may be looked on as evidence of the great
antiquity occasionally assigned to these ruins. Finally,
it may be remarked, that before their conversion to
Buddhism, the Kashmiris were Hindus, and after
adopting Buddhism, they continually relapsed into their
old ways. In Kashmir the oldest temples, if not ex-
clusively Naga, devoted to snake-worship, show an un-
mistakable tendency in that direction, and continued to
do so till the Hindu revival in the 11th century. After
that they were dedicated to Siva and Vishnu, and the
people in the valley were completely converted to the
Hindu religion. After that they fell under the influence of the Muhammadans, and adopted their faith
in the 14th century. It is between the fall of Buddhism and the rise of Muhammadanism that all the
temples in the true Kashmiri style must be ranged.

Before that there is nothing, after that only the tomb of Zeni-ul-ud-din, and the temple on the Tukht-i-Suleiman, in Srinagar, can be classed as examples of the style, though the latter can hardly even claim a title to that affiliation.

Having thus settled, as far as the opinions of the learned in such matters may be taken, the question of the Kashmiri style of architecture, the visitor will land at Avantipore and look at the fine ruins there with a more experienced eye than he might, perhaps, otherwise have been able. Avantipore, the residence of Avantiverma, the first king of the Utpala dynasty, was also the capital city, and there are ruins which show that it was an important place. Avantiverma was a devoted follower of Siva, and reigned from A.D. 875 to 904. It was during his reign that this temple, second only to Martand, was built. The two principal ruins stand in courtyards of nearly the same size, about 200 feet by 170 feet. One, called Avantiswain, is surrounded by pillars, like Martand, and in design and dimension is almost identical. The other is Astylar, or without columns. The temple at Avantipore has greater richness of detail than that at Martand. The pillars are beautiful,—they have been compared with those of the tomb of Mycene in Greece. It is affirmed that there is nothing between Greece and Kashmir that so nearly resembles the beautiful specimen of work found on these pillars. In 1865 the late Bishop Cotton caused some excavations to be made, which expose some very interesting remains and show the design of the building. The tributaries of the Jhelum are numerous near its source. The largest is the Veshan, which joins it on the left bank, a few hours after leaving Avantipore. Veshan rises in the lake called Konsa Nag on the top of a mountain near the Pir Panjal pass.

After passing the Veshan, the town of Bijbihara, a corruption of *Vidya Vehara*, or the Temple of Wisdom, is seen. It is built on the top of the river bank which at this spot is unusually high. An old wooden bridge is thrown across. There is a story told that an old Hindu temple stood here which Sikander, the bigoted Muhammadan king, destroyed, and used the stones to build a mosque. To be revenged Maharajah Golab Singh threw down the mosque, and built a temple out of the ruins. Above the bridge are the remains of a fine old pleasure garden laid out by the Moguls. It occupies both sides of the river, and though but small traces exist of it now, the plane trees, which are remarkably fine, show where the garden was. There are the remains, too, of a stone bridge which connected the two gardens. There is a Hindu temple in the town, and also a *ziarat*, a sacred spot, as every *ziarat* is. A large hole in the town is pointed out as the spot where the mosque stood which Maharajah Golab Singh destroyed. In the short distance between this town and Khanabal, the river Liddar joins the Jhelum. It flows down the Liddar valley, at the head of which is the famous mountain Amarnath, some 16,000 feet high. On the top is a cave, a spot sacred with the Hindus. A description of this cave is given further on. From Bijbihara there is an alternative route to Amarnath, joining the route from Islamabad, at Pahalgam. The river Liddar divides into two streams close to its junction with the Jhelum, and the

two mouths, each of which is as large as the Jhelum at
this part, may be seen close to Khanbal. The Jhelum
rapidly narrows here. At Khanbal it is a very small
stream, and a little higher up it ceases to be navigable :
Khanbal is a village about one mile from Islamabad.
Coolies may be engaged here, and arrangements made
for proceeding in three or four directions. There is a
rest-house by the river side, where the accommodation is
similar to that met with at other places in the valley.
There is a wooden bridge over the river. The visitor
will receive great attention from an individual named
Lassu Kotwal, whose innumerable and much-prized chits
may afford some amusement. Islamabad, called Anant
Nag by the Hindus, is a large town, similar as regards
its squalid appearance and dilapidated streets to Srinagar. The traveller sees more of this town than he
does of Srinagar, not from choice, but because he
must pass through some of the streets. It stands at
the foot of a conical hill, which is seen from nearly
every part of the valley. Adjoining is a wide, flat
piece of land about six miles long, a huge rice-field.
The most interesting object in the town is the residence
of the Maharajah. He visits Islamabad on his way
to or returning from Srinagar. He travels by the
Banhal route, and visits the sacred spring of Bawan.
Near the palace is the Sirkari Bagh, and within it is the
Anant Nag, significant of the ancient worship of the
people. The water of the Anant Nag flows from the
foot of the mountain. At this spot is a large tank
filled with fish, which the Hindus regard as sacred ; they
feed them and never allow one to be taken. There is
also a Kashmir water-mill for grinding flour. The

stones are very massive, and large quantities of wheat
are ground. Two or three other springs here are called
Nags. Slaik Nag issues from a fissure, and is pure and
fresh. Another, Malak Nag, bubbles up in the form of a
small fountain, and is strongly sulphurous. The Maharajah's garden is not kept in good order, especially
around the house set apart for the ladies of His Highness's household.   There are several Muhammadan
mosques in Islamabad; its productions are shawls,
saddle cloths, rugs, and cotton goods.

After leaving Islamabad, the visitor will doubtless
first march to Bawan and perhaps proceed beyond up
the Liddar valley to Amarnath; but he will more
probably visit Martand and thence to Achibal, leaving
the ascent of Amarnath to some other time, as that is a
matter of tedious marches up a mountain and requires
special preparations. Leaving Islamabad, then the
visitor will march for Bawan, five miles. The road
after a short distance runs at the foot of the mountains
on the right, on the sides of which may be seen several
peculiar beach-like levels, as though formerly water
washed over them. It is considered that these beaches,
which may be seen elsewhere in the valley, mark the
height of the water when the entire valley was a vast
lake, and that it fell from time to time, as the water
made its way out of the valley at the western end at
Baramulla, forming the lower beaches. The quantity of
shingle found on these beaches and in the valley just
below the mountains, is also taken as an indication of the
existence at some early period of a large body of water.

Bawan is one of the most delightful spots in
Kashmir. Here there is a grove of very large plane

trees, so close together that to go under them is like entering some dark building, so effectually is the light of the sun excluded. Here tents can be pitched and a delightful cool retreat secured. Close by is a Hindu temple enclosing a large tank which abounds with fish The water issues from this tank and rushes in a cool, clear, wholesome torrent under the plane trees, and is lost in the river below. The ground under these trees looks as if formerly a large garden had been laid out ; some of the stone channels for water still remain, and stone walls which support the embankment on which the plane trees stand.

A mile from Bawan are two curious caves, which the natives consider to have been specially created for some mysterious purpose. Consequently they are places of pilgrimage. They are called Bhumjoo. The long cave is about 40 feet up the side of the mountain, which is a confused mass of rocks. After climbing over some of these, an entrance is suddenly seen. A torch brought from Bawan is lighted, and the cave is entered At first the passage is easy, but water drops from the roof; then the passage becomes narrow and low, till, after proceeding about 200 feet further, progress is stopped by the way being narrowed so as not to admit any one further. In a chamber on one side, not far from the entrance, are the bones of some devotee who terminated his career at this spot. On looking at the mountain from the outside of the cave, it will be noticed that the course of the passage in the cave is along the lower part of the mountain ; water possibly forced a way into an aperture there may be at the further end of the cave and made the passage ; and in

all likelihood many similar caves would be found if the
water in some of the sulphurous springs were to suddenly cease running. A little further on, in the same
mountain, is a Hindu temple inside a cave. It is called
the Temple Cave. The entrance is about 100 feet from
the ground, to which there is a wooden flight of stairs.
The entrance is a trefoil arch; the interior is oval; at
the upper end is a Hindu shrine. There is a fine view
from the top of the stairs of part of the Liddar river
and valley. There is a *ziarat* below the temple.

The ruins of *Martand* are close to Bawan, about 1½
miles distant, up a slight ascent to the top of a lovely
plain, and commanding the most charming views. As
Achibal is an easy march from Bawan, the better plan
is to visit Martand on the march, as those ruins must
be passed on the road to Achibal.

The ruins of Martand, or the Temple of the Sun, have
been pronounced by competent authority to be the
finest and most typical example of the Kashmiri style.
The position occupied, alone in its grandeur, with
neither tree nor house near, and on an elevated plateau
overlooking a large part of the valley, is very impressive.
The temple is 60 feet long and 38 feet wide; its height,
when complete, was 60 feet. The width of the façade
was eked out by two wings or adjuncts, which make it
60 feet. "It thus realises the problem the Jews so
earnestly set themselves to solve, how to build a temple
with the three dimensions equal, but yet not a cube
Small, however, as the Jewish temple was, it was more
than twice as large as this one. At Jerusalem
the temple was 150 cubits, or 150 feet in length,
breadth, and height. At Martand these dimensions

were only 60 feet. But it is one of the points of interest in the Kashmiri temple that it reproduces, in plan at least, the Jewish temple more nearly than any other known temple." The above quotation is from Fergusson's " Indian and Eastern Architecture, "and it gives a true estimate of the Martand temple. The roof was probably of wood, for the walls were probably not strong enough to support a stone roof. The Buddhists frequently used wood in the roofs of their *chaitya* halls, and it is considered that wood was used when this temple was erected.

The courtyard that surrounds and encloses the temple, is a more remarkable object than the temple itself. Its internal dimensions are 220 by 142 feet. On each face is a central cell, larger and higher than the colonnade in which it is placed. The height is 30 feet, and the pillars on each side are 9 feet high, not lofty certainly, but they have a Grecian aspect which is interesting. It is thought that the whole of the interior of the quadrangle was originally filled with water to a level within one foot of the bases of the columns, and that access to the temple was gained by a raised pathway of slabs, supported on solid blocks at short intervals, which connected the gateway flight of steps with that leading to the temple. The same kind of pathway stretched right across the quadrangle from one side doorway to the other. In Shalimar and other gardens pathways of this sort are met with. A constant supply of fresh water was kept up from the river Lambadari, which was conducted alongside the mountain for the service of the village of Sinbarotsika close by. Other temples in Kashmir stand in water, the object being to place them more immediately under the protection of the Nagas or human bodies and snake-tailed gods, who were jealously worshipped for ages throughout Kashmir.

The time when the enclosure at Martand was erected is believed, by some, to be during the reign of Lalita-ditya (A.D. 725-761). General Cunningham, however, on the strength of a passage in the " Rajtarangini," ascribes the building of the temple to Ranaditya, who reigned from A.D. 578 to 594. Mr. Fergusson, never-theless, doubts the correctness of this opinion, and does not consider it to be clear that it is dedicated to the sun. He also thinks that it was probably built about 100 years after the temple at Avantipore, about A.D. 852 or 853, and not so long as 250 years before.

The visitor may return to Islamabad from here if he wishes, but there is no advantage in doing so, and the road from Achibal to Islamabad has no special attrac-tions.

Leaving these ruins, the march to Achibal across the plateau lies over an easy level road. The scenery in every direction is extremely striking and pretty. The road after a mile or so makes a sudden descent to the valley of the river Arpal, which is crossed over a bridge. The adjoining land is cultivated for rice, and the path through the rice-fields is sometimes swampy, but further on the road rises again, and there is a charming walk to Achibal. This is one of the prettiest places in Kashmir. There is a very good rest-house in the barrack form, but the front is awkwardly placed for getting a view therefrom of the surrounding country. There are some fine plane trees opposite, under which tents may be pitched, and the village is close by. The old pleasure garden at Achibal, which was laid out by orders of the Emperor Jehangir, is preserved with some care by the Maharajah. The summer-house is in good order, and the garden is enclosed in a high wall. The water that runs through the garden and supplies the fountains and waterfalls, flows from beneath the mountain at the back of the garden. At times it gurgles up from beneath with great force ; it is one of several streams of water proceeding from beneath the same mountain, and is perhaps the Bringh river, which disappears suddenly on the opposite side of this mountain ; the other streams may be seen a few hundred yards distant near the village. The visitor will notice the beautiful belt of country entered on at Achibal. It is adorned with several low ranges of hills, all of which are covered with plenty of shrubs and similar undergrowth, with numerous ravines affording good food and shelter for bear and deer. Rich and fertile valleys divide these low ranges from each other, and there are many mountain streams running through them, and more rain falls in this part of the valley than in the more open spaces. Marching direct from Vernag to Islamabad, the extent of these lower ranges may be easily perceived ; they terminate a few miles westward of Vernag, and the richness of their valleys is in very perceptible contrast to the open and less fertile land on the rest of the march to Islamabad

Leaving Achibal the visitor may march to Vernag, 15 miles distant. The road runs for some miles at the foot of a low range of hills, on which there is plenty of good shooting, and then joins the high road from Jammu to Islamabad, over the Banhal pass.

There is a longer route from Vernag to Achibal. The first march is from *Achibal to Naobog, 12 miles.* The road passes through Changas, four miles from Achibal. This place is in the valley, of which such a beautiful view can be obtained from Achibal. Running through is a stream which rises near the foot of the *Morgon pass,* about 11,000 feet in height, over which is the road into the Wardwan valley. The shooting in the mountains is good. The next march is from *Naobog to Kookar Nag,* 12 *miles.* The shortest of the two roads is by the village of Sof, between two and three miles from Kookar. Iron is found in the surrounding mountains, and other metals are said to exist there. Copper is reported to have been found in State territory in the valley, but no attempt to work it has yet been made.

On this march the valley of the Bringh river is entered about seven miles from Naobog by a bridge, near which is the *musjid* of Hajee Daud Sahib, and here the road to Kishtwar is joined. At Kookar Nag is another of the numerous springs issuing from the mountain. Here the water flows from several springs; it is very cold, and is reported to have exhilarating and health-giving properties.

The next march is from *Kookar Nag to Vernag, about* 8 *miles.* The road ascends over the range of hills to the village of Noroo, about two miles from Kookar Nag. Of the two roads thence to Vernag, it is advisable to take the longer, that being much more agreeable than the other, which is usually used by the coolies. Shaha-bad, through which the longer road passes, was formerly

a favorite residence of some of the rulers of Kashmir,
but it is now in a very reduced and dilapidated
condition.

Vernag is very prettily situated at the foot of a
mountain covered with dense undergrowth and pines.
The Maharajah's summer-house in the garden is set
apart for visitors. It is large, and its spacious rooms
afford accommodation for many travellers at one time.
In the octagonal tank behind the house are thousands
of fish. Here also is a pleasure garden laid out by the
Emperor Jehangir, or more probably by his wife Nur
Mehal, who without doubt selected the beautiful spots
for these gardens and designed them. The Emperor
was too indolent to trouble himself about such matters.
The water flows into a huge octagonal stone tank more
than 100 feet wide and about 50 feet deep. It then
runs into the Sandrahan river, and thence to the
Bringh. Both rivers join the Jhelum a little above
the Kanbal.

The Emperor Jehangir, when dying, desired to be
carried to this spot, but he never reached it, his death
taking place at Bahramgul on the Pir Panjal route. On
a wall in the interior is the following inscription :—

" Az Jehangir Shah Akbar Shah,
In bina sar kashid bar aflak,
Buneh akl zaft tarikash
Kansarabad u Chashmahe Vernag."

The translation runs.—" This place was raised to the
skies by Jehangir Shah Akbar Shah. Consider well,
its date is found in the words ' Palace of the fountain
of Vernag.' "

By adding up the numerical values of the letters in
the above phrase, the date 1029 A.H., or 1619 A.D.,
is arrived at.

Having seen the source of the Jhelum at Vernag, the
visitor can, if he has no objection to six more marches,
some of them tedious, and the scenery throughout the
first three being very similar to that on the last three
marches, return to Srinagar by way of Rozloo and
Shupyan ; or he can return to Islamabad, and thence,
leaving at sunset, reach Srinagar the following morning.
There is a cataract at Haribal, on the fourth march,
which ought to be visited ; but that can be easily seen
from Shupyan. A description of it will be found in
the chapter in which the marches to Srinagar by the
Pir Panjal route are given. Below are a few details of
the six marches above referred to.

Vernag to Rozloo, 8 miles.— The road runs close to the
foot of the Pir Panjal range, and is moderately level.
Rozloo valley is also at the foot of this range, and there
is plenty of pretty scenery.

Rozloo to Ban Doosar, 11 miles.—The scenery is fine
throughout ; the road enters the plains, passing through
a large village, called Saogaum, three miles further
through Pet Doosar, and finally four miles further, to
Dan Doosar, on the banks of a small stream. There is
no rest-house here.

Ban Doosar to Nohan, 11 miles.—On this march the
river Vishan is crossed ; it is a considerable stream,
and spreads out over a wide space, with a loose stony
bottom. A large village, called Koolgaum, with two
ziarats on the side of a *karewah*, is passed after marching three miles. The road then descends and follows

the valley of the Vishan, to Nohan, a small village on the left bank of the river.

Nohan to Shupyan, either 9 or 13 miles, there being two roads. The longest road leads to the cataract at Haribal. Both marches are fairly easy.

Shupyan to Srinagar, 2 marches, 11 and 18 miles.— These marches have already been described.

The Liddar is a beautiful valley with magnificent scenery on all sides. It is traversed by the river Liddar, which has its origin in glaciers. The river is formed below Pahalgam by the junction of two tributaries, the Kolahoi and Shishram Nag. The famous cave of Amarnath, a sacred place of Hindu pilgrimage, lies up the Liddar. The pilgrim route passes Bawan and the village of Aishmukam. A few miles from this village is Ganeshbal. About two miles further on is the beautiful spot called Pahalgam, where there is a good camping ground. From Pahalgam the road goes to Tanin, 12 miles, altitude 10,500 feet above sea level. The path is rough, but practicable for ponies and *jhampans.* The march from Tanin to Shishram Nag (13,000 feet) is a stiff climb of 11 miles. Panchatarani is the same distance, but a pass 14,000 feet above sea level has to be crossed. The cave of Amarnath is five miles distant from Panchatarani. The cave, which lies in a hollow of Gypsum rock, is about 50 yards long. The width at the mouth is 50 yards, narrowing to 30 in the centre. It is about 30 yards high. On the return journey pilgrims descend, *via* Hatyartala and Astranmarg. The traveller should make all the necessary arrangements for supplies and coolies at Bawan. The coolies should be engaged for the whole journey.

Beyond Pahalgam the scenery is magnificent. The stages can also be taken as follows.

Pilgrim Route from Islamabad to Amarnath.

Name of stage.	Miles.	Remarks.
Islamabad to Aishmu-kam	12	Supplies plentiful. Road good. On the way halt at Bawan, two miles from Martand.
Pahalgam ...	12	Supplies plentiful. Road good.
Chandanwari	8	No supplies. Road very rough. Country uninhabited.
Shishram Nag	7	Road steep. No fuel.
Panchatarani	8	Ascent gradual. Five shallow streams have to be crossed.
Amarnath	4½	The famous cave, which is supposed to be the dwelling-place of a Shiva of ice, is reached by ascending Bairaunath, and then descending by a steep path.

CHAPTER VI.

WESTERN PORTION OF THE VALLEY.

FROM SRINAGAR DOWN THE RIVER JHELUM.

LEAVING Srinagar for the western end of the valley, many pleasant days may be spent in visiting several places of interest on the route. There is no difficulty to encounter, and the boats float quietly down the stream, the boatmen occasionally plying their *chappas*, but more frequently doing little or no work. If a quicker passage is desired, the boats can be towed from the bank. But in the summer it is delightful to float slowly along, stopping now and then at some shady spot on the banks for breakfast or lunch. The usual busy scene is witnessed on either side of the river as the boat passes under the seven bridges at Srinagar. Cherub-like children bathing, laughing and playing, the mothers fetching water, and the *khisties* plying up and down the stream, make a lively picture. The dilapidated houses on each bank of the river, the broken stairs to the water's edge, the ruins of the old stone walls once protecting the banks, and the quaint wooden bridges, fill up the scene, which is one of the most remarkable and exceptional that even an experienced traveller has beheld. As soon as the last bridge is passed, the river expands into a very wide stream, and maintains its breadth for a long way. A little below this bridge, on the left, the Dudhganga river falls into the Jhelum; and about a mile further on is a landing place whence the march to Pattan and Gulmarg

may be commenced.   Servants and horses may be sent
round to this spot by a short cut.   About a mile below
the last bridge on the left bank of the river is a fine
grove of poplars called Purana Chowni or Kripa
Ram's Chowni.   Further down the river, on the right
bank, is a grove of chinars called *Sonar Boni* or the
Goldsmith's Chinars.   The Maharajah usually camps
here for breakfast before his arrival at Srinagar.   The
hill of Gulmarg will be pointed out by the boatmen on
the left.   The round hill overlooking Manesbal lake
meets the eye all the way to Shadipore on the right,
and beyond as far as Sambal.   A little beyond Sambal,
on the right, is a canal, about a mile long, which
connects the Jhelum with lake Manesbal.

Shadipore may be reached in about four hours.   At
this place the river Sindh joins the Jhelum.   It is a
fine, broad stream, nearly as wide as the Jhelum, and
brings down a large body of water.   At the point of
junction, or perhaps, where some time ago the Sindh
river flowed into the Jhelum, is a large plane tree, the
roots carefully protected by a stone wall, in the form of
a square; on the top is a *lingam*, which is an object of
worship to the Hindus.   The union of the two rivers is
signified in the name of the place Shadipore, which
means the town of marriage.   Some Hindu devotees
are reported to have immolated themselves at the spot
in the river where a chinar tree stands.   Similar stories
are told of immolations at the Haribal cataract, a more
probable place for the performance of this last grand
act of devotion than the chinar tree at Shadipore.   The
" Rajtarangini," a history of Kashmir, which has been
called the only Indian history in existence, states, how-

ever, that the Dewan of the greatest ruler in Kashmir, Lalitaditya, threw himself into the waters here.

From Shadipore the Sindh river may be ascended as far as Gandarbal, whence the Sindh valley is reached. A description of this route is given elsewhere. On the left the Noroo canal joins the Jhelum. There is a bridge over this canal at Shadipore. It is at this junction that the principal portion of the town stands. The canal is the work of the Moguls. It is very useful for the conveyance of traffic to Sopur without going through the Wular lake, on which terrible storms of wind frequently occur during the summer months, when the surface of the lake is too rough for the flat-bottomed Kashmir boats. There is a story of some adventurous Sikh ruler going on the lake, accompanied by some 300 boats, when one of these storms came on, swamping the greater number, and endangering the safety of the ruler himself; many lives were lost on that occasion. The canal avoids risks of this sort. The water is spread out on either side this canal, which seems really to be a pathway through immense quantities of the *singara* plant, which grows hereabouts and covers miles of water that otherwise would be open. The depth of water in the canal is greater than elsewhere.

A little below Shadipore, on the right, is a pleasure garden, which was laid out in 1820 by Surij Bahri, a minister of Motiram, the first Governor of Kashmir under Ranjit Singh. The garden, which is a short distance from the river bank, and which was kept in very good order when Baron Hugel visited it in 1835, is now uncared for, and utterly neglected.

At Sambal, a small place, about two hours journey below Shadipore, there is a bridge over the Jhelum. On each side of the river, near the bridge, are some very fine chinar trees. Below the bridge the fishing is good. The camping ground is good also, and snipe shooting can be had in the swamps near Sambal. Not far down the broad stream, on the right, will be seen a canal, which takes the traveller to Manesbal lake, a really lovely spot and the most charming lake in Kashmir. A short distance up this canal is an old, stone bridge with a very high arch, built in that form to be clear of the highest floods of the Jhelum, which will sometimes rise so high as to render the passage under the arch, lofty as it is, impossible. But the surrounding land being covered with water, boats can go round the bridge and make a straight passage to the lake, the course of the canal being obliterated. This old bridge is the work of the Moguls. One of the stones near the low level of the water is evidently taken from some Hindu temple. Similar stones are met with occasionally in secluded spots in the valley. They are often put under a big tree, and a circle made round them. The figures thereon, which are smeared over with red ochre, are worshipped.

Manesbal lake, which is in the form of an oblong, three miles by one mile, is at the end of the slightly tortuous canal. In many parts the water is over 40 feet deep. The lake lies north-east and south-west between a low range of hills on the right. A lofty mountain over-shadows the further end. On the left, on the north side, there are two or three little villages, near which the lotus, held so sacred by the Hindus, grows in abundance, covering a large piece of water, and in July, when in full flower, presenting a really lovely appearance. A dozen of these really beautiful flowers will partly fill a small *kisti*. Such a nosegay is very rarely seen, and only once a year even at Manesbal. The lotus water-lily (*Nymphæa lotus*) will also be seen in the neighbourhood in abundance. It is a much smaller flower, with yellow leaves. Manesbal lake was another of those spots in the vale of Kashmir so well selected by the Emperor Jehangir's " Light of the Harem," the beautiful Nur Mehal, on which to erect a pleasure house and lay out a garden. On the north side will be seen the remains of the Badshah Bagh, or rather of thehouse only ; the bagh is now a large rice-field The water that formerly ran over the water-falls of the garden, the remains of which are visible, and fell into the lake, now is used to irrigate the land on which the rice is grown. At the head of the lake, some 50 feet up the high bank, is a small grove of chinar trees, under which is a delightful though small en-camping ground. There is close by a house in which lives a curious old Muhammadan *fakir*, who has em-ployed part of his time during the last twenty years in enlarging the spot he has chosen in the side of the hill for his grave, till it is now some 50 or 60 feet long. Around his house are several fruit trees ; in the early summer cherries are in abundance, and later on excel-lent peaches, famous for miles round, are gathered from his trees The high mountain at the head of the lake is part of a range running up the Sindh valley, part of which may be seen from Manesbal. Over the rounded side of the low hill immediately on the lake, at the gap

on the eastern end, the water falls in copious streams
into the lake from the mountain springs at the top.
Below is the ruin of a Hindu temple, probably the roof,
the rest of the building being buried in the mud and
silt collected in past ages. In the village opposite
are some State lime-kilns, where lime is prepared and
sent to Srinagar for building and other purposes. Lime,
which abounds in this part of the valley, has been
taken from here ever since the days of the Moguls.
The water in the streams on the opposite side of the
lake runs white with lime mixed with it. Half-way
between Badshah and the lime-kilns the water is 40
feet deep, but it gets to 50 feet about quarter of a mile
from the shore to the west of Badshah, at the foot of
a spur running down to the edge of the lake. Altogether
Manesbal is a really delightful spot. The breeze
from the east blows gently in the morning through the
gap, and in the evening from the other end of the lake.
In the hottest time of the year Manesbal is pleasant,
and during the rains, clear, bright days with light clouds
frequently occur, when dark, heavy clouds are resting
on Gulmarg and Sonamarg, west and east, and
pouring torrents of rain day after day on those un-
happy hills. The mosquitoes at Manesbal at sunset in
the damp weather are very troublesome; but they can
be avoided more readily than can the incessant rains
elsewhere. There is not much shade at Manesbal,
except at the head of the lake, and there space for
camping is somewhat confined. There being no rest-
house, tents must be pitched. Manesbal is a very
healthy place, entirely free from the malaria which
arises about Srinagar in July and August, and for ladies

is a warmer and more desirable place in those months than Gulmarg and Sonamarg, which are several degrees colder.

Leaving Manesbal, the next object is to visit the *Wular lake*, which is the largest in India, but it must be supposed that the proper season has arrived for this purpose, the end of September or beginning of October, when the storms may be considered to have passed away. Then the Wular lake presents a fine expanse of water, backed by a range of mountains which partly encircles the lake, and then turns abruptly to the west. The water is said to be 16 feet deep opposite the hill called Shukarudin, and about 8 to 12 feet in other places. When on the lake, it is easy to understand the effect of heavy gusts of wind, for the surface of the water in the early morning in autumn is soon ruffled by the gentle morning breezes which continue for an hour or two. At this time and in the cold weather immense quantities of wild ducks and geese will be seen, and some excellent shooting may be had, and if a long gun be used in a boat fitted for the purpose, the usual mode of shooting adopted by the Kashmiris, several may be shot at one time. The ducks are very good eating, and may be bought as many as are required for a very small sum, five or six for one rupee. In winter, during severe frosts, the lake is frozen over and navigation is impossible. There is an island, or *lanka*, at the entrance to the lake, where there are some ruins, but the approach is difficult owing to the quantity of *singara* plants around it. The ruins are those of a Hindu building, not unlike those at Martand, with two rows' of trefoil arches.

There is also a brick building at the north-western corner, and an inscription, from which it appears that the *lanka* was constructed by a Muhammadan ruler, Zinal-ab-udin, in A.D. 1411. There are on the north side several ruined pillars, some of which are handsomely carved, but on others the carving is not so distinct. The remains of the Hindu temple would indicate that the *lanka* had been in the lake long before A.D. 1411. It is probable that the temple was erected at an early period on a very small island, which the Muhammadans afterwards enlarged.

On the north-east of the Wular lake is the rising town of Bandipore, which is the starting point for the march to Gures, Skardu, and Gilgit. The lofty Haramuk is two marches across the mountains from Bandipore. Its height is 16,905 feet above sea level, and on its summit is the small lake of Gungabal, which is held very sacred by the Hindus. Indeed, in August, every Kashmiri Pundit, who has lost any relatives during the year, deposits their bones in its waters. The marches to Skardu and Gilgit are given elsewhere. Before leaving the Wular lake, the hill of Shukarudin may perhaps be visited. It is plainly visible on the western side, a very prominent spur about 700 feet high. It may be easily ascended from the southern side. A *ziarat* is on the top, in which are the remains of Baba Shukarudin; the view of the lake from the summit is very complete, embracing, besides the lake, the hills on either side, Gulmarg and an extensive view of the valley.

Sopur is the next point of interest; it is a dilapidated place on both sides of the Jhelum, connected by a bridge, partly stone and partly wooden. This place has been already noticed in the Murree route. There is some excellent mahseer fishing here. Sopur is the starting place for Gulmarg or the Lolab valley.

From Sopur to Gulmarg.—This route is preferred to any other, as it involves less fatigue, the distance being only about 18 miles, or one day's march. There are really two marches, one to Kontur, 13 miles, an easy road, and the other five miles to Gulmarg. At the village of Naupore the pony road from Baramulla is met with, and at Kontur the footpath from that place Joins. Kontur is a village on the hill side, command-ing a view of the Ningil valley. There is no rest-house. From Kontur to Gulmarg the road, after crossing a small stream several times, leads by an easy ascent of about two miles to the foot of the mountain, and thence to Gulmarg on the top, through Baba Mirishi. This place contains a famous *ziarat*, much frequented and venerated by Muhammadans, who come here in large numbers once a week in the summer. Here is buried Baba Pyoomdin, a *rishi* or saint, who died some 400 years ago. The other route to Gulmarg, which is sometimes taken, is from Srinagar to Palhalan by boat, *via* Shadipore, and thence through Baba Mirishi. There is a small rest-house at Pattan. At Baba Mirishi there is another, but the latter is only a large room of wood raised on brick supports three or four feet above the ground. The view is remarkably good and very extensive, as the elevation is considerably above the valley, the road for a few miles rising rapidly through the forest to Baba Mirishi.

All the ascents of the mountain, on the top of which is Gulmarg, are steep, but an easy road leads up from Baba Mirishi. The sides are covered with a dense forest which testifies to the large quantity of rain that falls there, and the path up is frequently well drenched with the water pouring down. At Baba Mirishi there is less rain in July and August than at Gulmarg; and on that account visitors sometimes remain at the former place, but the camping ground is limited.

The following are the principal routes to Gulmarg :—,

(1.) From Baramulla, *viâ* Kontur and Baba Mirishi. The distance is 19 miles, and the road good, though rather steep in places. Visitors arriving in Kashmir in the middle of the season, and intending to proceed direct to Gulmarg, should take this route.

(2.) From Sopur, *viâ* Naupore to Kontur, and thence *viâ* Baba Mirishi. The distance is 23 miles.

(3.) From Srinagar by land all the way *viâ* Magam. The distance is covered in two marches. There is a dilapidated rest-house at Magam, from which place Gulmarg is 12 miles distant. The starting point for this route may be below Srinagar at Shalateng, which can be reached from the Munshi Bagh in two hours by boat. From here the Baramulla-Srinagar road is followed for a short distance, and then a winding and fatiguing path leads to Magam.

(4.) From Srinagar by boat to Palhalan, and thence *viâ* Baba Mirishi. The boat journey takes about eight hours. From Palhalan to Gulmarg is 17 miles.

(5.) From Srinagar, *viâ* Khandhama, 23 miles.

(6) From Srinagar to Pattan by the Baramulla-Srinagar road, and thence *viâ* Baba Mirishi.

(7) From Naushera to Gulmarg. Between Rampor and Baramulla is a little village called Naushera, from where there is a steep and rough path leading up to Gulmarg.

Gulmarg is the favourite resort of visitors to Kashmir during the height of the summer. The season, which begins in the middle of June, lasts for about three months. Huts are available on the first-come-first-served principle. Nedou's hotel has removed many inconveniences which· formerly were experienced. It is very comfortable and well managed. During the season, when the Resident is at Gulmarg, a bazar is opened, and requisites of every kind are to be found at the Srinagar branch shops, which are also open then. Babu Amar Nath, at Srinagar, will furnish coolies, etc., on application. At Gulmarg there is a race course, cricket ground, and lawn-tennis courts. Gymkhanas and all kinds of festivities make the short season there a pleasant one. But for these attractions visitors would perhaps prefer the better climate of Sonamarg, or the bracing air and magnificent views of Gures or Pahalgam. The climate is bracing, but the drainage of the Marg itself is defective. Gulmarg means literally a flowery meadow, and a veritable flowery meadow it is. Its height above the level of the sea is about 8,500 feet. Snow falls at the end of October, and during the winter it lies many feet thick. A few miles from Gulmarg, and about 2,000 feet above it, is another Marg called Khillan. From Khillan, the mountain of Apharwat, about 14,000 feet high, may be visited. A glacier on

the south-east of Khillan is also worth seeing. At
Gulmarg there are many varieties of flowers and ferns ;
some of the flowers are very beautiful ; many of them
have been copied on the *papier maché* work of Kashmir. For rules about houses at Gulmarg, see Appendix.
As heavy rain often falls for several days and nights,
visitors should consider the propriety of passing the
wet season at Gulmarg if good house accommodation is
not available.

Vigne thus describes Gulmarg.— " A lovely spot on
the downs of the Punjal, flat, green, open, and perfumed'
with wild flowers ; the snowy peaks sloping gently up-
wards from its extremities, and the valley itself extended
beneath it, whilst the scenic disposition of its woods
and glades, watered by a stream that winds through its
whole length from north-west to south-east, is so highly
picturesque, tbat little is wanting but a mansion and a
herd of deer to complete its resemblance to an English
park. Its length may be about one mile and a half,
and its width, which is varied, for its shape is tri-
angular, about one third of a mile at the widest part. At
the end is a bank over the stream, on which it is said
that the Emperor Jehangir and his celebrated Nur
Jehan pitched their tents when indulging in a pic-nic,
and at the furthest extremity is a steep descent through
the jungle, by a path which joins the pass named
after the village of Firuzpur, which lies at its foot.
The vast mountain of Nunga Parbat is seen to great
effect from the ascent to the Gulmarg."

Returning to Sopur from Gulmarg, the next place to
visit is the Lolab valley, and this may be done from
Sopur, or by the river Pohra. However, the Sopur

route is the usual one. Lalpura is the principal place in the valley, but it is hardly more than a village. There are many small villages, all of them prettily situated, and supplies are easily obtained. The far-famed beauty of the Kashmiri women is reported to be seen in some of these villages, but the traveller may form his own opinion as to the correctness of this report. The climate is very delightful, and the marches are easy. The most direct route is from Sopur to Arwan, and thence to Lalpura, about 17 miles, along a level, prettv road. At Arwan are some iron works. From Arwan the ascent is rather steep, but from the top a full view of the lovely valley of the Lolab is obtained.

The route to the Lolab valley by the Pohra river is very pleasant, but the water in this river is very low at times. It can, however, be ascended from May to September. The Pohra river is a few hours' delightful journey by boat from Sopur ; the views on either side the Jhelum are varied and charming. At the village of Duogao, at the junction of the Pohra with the Jhelum, there is a beautiful grove of plane trees, and here is the hop garden. By four hours' journey in a boat up the Pohra, from Dubgao, Jseda Kak ka Bagh is reached. Thence a level path of four miles leads to Arwan. Ascending the Pohra, about 20 hours from Dubgao by boat, is Awatkoola, a village on the left bank ; here the stream is very strong, and some difficulty is sometimes experienced in getting along. The Lolab valley lies on the other side of the low range of hills, which run a long distance near the river. There is a road to Lalpura over this range, but it is steep, and about 12 miles long. Kofwara is a village which may be reached from here; it is on the Lolah river, and there is a thick forest near it, through which the road passes.

The Lolab valley abounds with bears; they consume large quantities of fruit, and may be heard in the walnut trees cracking the walnuts during the night. The sound when first heard is surprising, and difficult to find whence it comes, till the discovery of bruin at his repast settles the question. From Lalpura the traveller can return by Alsoo and Kewnas to Sopur, and thence to Baramulla, if he intends to leave the valley by the Murree route.

The Sindh Valley.—A visit to this lovely valley will doubtless be made a separate excursion. If taken after visiting the Lolab valley, the traveller will rejoin his boats at Sopur, and proceed to Shadipore, and thence ascend the river Sindh. The first place visited will be Gandarbal, about four hours' journey by boat. Gandarbal is fourteen miles from Srinagar. The road runs past the fort and through the village of Naushera. Between these places are the ruins at Zoribal. Lake Anchar is passed and several streams of water. One of these streams runs a short distance underground. At Malshabagh there are beach remains, similar to those seen near Bawan in the Liddar valley, and which indicate the former existence of the huge lake which geologists consider once filled the entire valley of Kashmir. In the summer, when there is plenty of water in the Dal lake and in the canal, boats can pass through the Nalla Mar canal and emerge on the Anchar lake beyond. Across this expanse of water

the Sindh river is entered by a branch which runs into
the Anchar and thence to Gandarbal. By this route
Gandarbal may be reached in about six hours from
Srinagar.

Gandarbal is situated at the junction of a small
stream with the Sindh river. During the season there is
a great rush of water here. The remains of an old
stone bridge marks the divergence of the Sindh river
since its erection, for it stands partly away from the
main channel now. It was probably a long bridge of
perhaps ten or twelve arches. The ruins are very
massive, and the bridge, though a long one, was not very
wide. It is another monument of Mogul enterprise.
On a large maidan, about a mile from this spot, is
a charming camping ground in a grove of fine plane
trees.

In the Sindh valley the scenery' comprises lofty
mountains, mostly covered with forests, stretching
down to the valley, at times nearly closing it, and
again opening ; many smaller valleys join it, and down
each rushes a mountain torrent, altogether forming
the Sindh river, which at times is very powerful, bring-
ing down big trees and logs of wood. The chief
objects of interest in the Sindh valley are the Wangat
ruins and Sonamarg. To the former there is a road
across the Sindh river from Gandarbal. To Sonamarg the first march is from Gandarbal to Kangan.
The time occupied is about five hours, and the distance
11 miles. The level road runs through a wide valley.
The mountains on the south side are barren, those on
the opposite side are covered with forests and undergrowth. This is the characteristic of all the marches.

It will be noticed that the valley narrows as one pro-
ceeds to the head at Gagangair.

The second march—14 miles—is from Kangan to
Gond. The mountains are more lofty, and in the
distance snow may be seen on some of the peaks. The
Sindh river is crossed twice, and its tributaries several
times. It is advisable for riders to dismount and have
their horses led across these streams.

In the third march from Gond to Gagangair—9
miles—the road rises in some places and again falls to the
level of the river, which rushes wildly along. The valley
closes in at the end of this march. There are a few
huts which are occupied in the summer. Horses may
be engaged here for the next march, which is a very
difficult one.

The fourth and last march from Gagangair to Sonamarg is about 10 miles, but as the path runs along the
rocky side of the mountain, the difficulties are sometimes great, the road rising and falling very suddenly.
The path passes at nearly right angles to the valley,
and the river runs in a narrow channel, the mountains
on either side coming down to its banks. The scenery
is wild and beautiful. The road passes through a forest
nearly all the way, and when the Sonamarg hill comes
in view, the mountains come down in places, like a wall,
one thousand feet, more or less. The river is then
crossed, but there is no bridge, and the ascent is made
of Sonamarg. This is not formidable. At about one
hundred feet above the river is a spot, overlooking the
river and a small village on its bank, where tents may be
conveniently pitched. This spot is sheltered from the
high winds which frequently sweep over the Marg.

The Marg is about 100 feet above this spot, and can be easily reached the day after arrival. Sonamarg is a plain surrounded by very lofty mountains; it is 8,500 feet above sea level. This plain extends for about two miles between the hill side and the river bank. There is adjoining a wider tract of undulating ground, with dells and hillocks, in and on which are numerous wild flowers. Fir, sycamore and birch trees are met with, and the scenery in the summer is very beautiful. Numerous bare mountains are seen in every direction, with huge rocks and lofty peaks, in each of the hollows,. between which may be seen glaciers, many stony slopes and moraines, composed of the detritus formed at the bases and edges of glaciers. Beneath these may be seen the birch forests, the bark from the trees of which supplies the *bhoj-putti* used in covering the roofs of houses in Srinagar and other places in the valley. Being a longer distance from Srinagar than Gulmarg, Sonamarg is not so often visited but it is a pleasanter place, with fine views not to be obtained from the large hollow round, in which the huts of Gulmarg stand rather sulkily. There was a wooden church erected here some time ago, but it was destroyed by fire, owing to part of the church being used by a traveller as a stable for his horses; the servants lighted a fire, and the whole build. ing was consumed. Sonamarg is on the road to Leh. Two marches from Sonamarg is Zojila, a pass 11,300 feet above sea level.

Wangat is about 18 miles from Gandarbal, and the ruins are nearly two miles further. These ruins are similar to those at Martand; they are situated in

marshy ground ; probably there was plenty of water
there at one time, thus bearing out the conjecture that
Martand and all similar temples in Kashmir originally
were surrounded by water. The Sindh river is crossed,
and the road leads up a valley at right-angles to the
Sindh valley, in the direction of the lofty mountain
Haramuk, which is seen towering above its surroundings, to the height of 16,905 feet above sea level. The
largest of the lakes on the slopes of Haramuk is Gangabal, a sacred lake. The ruined temples near Wangat
were doubtless built in connection with it. Gangabal is
visited annually, in the month of August, by a large
number of Hindus, who toil up the mountain with a
holy zeal similar to that which inspires them to visit
the icy cave on the summit of Amarnath in the Liddar
valley. This lake is said to be 1½ mile long and about
250 yards wide. The ruins near Wangat are called
Rajdainbal and Nagbal. They are near each other.
From Tronkul near Gangabal there is a route to Jabel,
a famous sporting ground. There are two roads to
Gangabal from Gandarbal ; the first crosses the Sindh
river a short distance from Gandarbal, and Wangal is
reached by two marches of about nine miles each. The
road is not good, being mainly used by coolies ; the
several bridges are very rudely constructed. The
second road is also two marches. Towards the end of
the second march the road runs along the side of a
steep mountain, and is dangerous in some places. The
first march is from Gandarbal to Kangan ; there the
Sindh valley is left and the river Kondnai, which runs
through the valley to Wangal and beyond, is seen, and
is crossed below Wangal, which is situated on the top

of a steep hill about 500 feet above. The view from
Wangal is varied and beautiful. The main obJect in
visiting Wangal is to see the ruins at Nara Nog, rather
less than five miles distant, in the midst of a dense
forest. These ruins consist of two groups of temples,
the first at Rajdainbal, nearest to Wangal ; the second
at Naghal, just beyond the first. The first group comprises a large temple, 24 feet square, with a projection
on each of its four sides, and five other buildings ; the
second consists of seven buildings, the principal one, 25
feet square, with projections on each face ; there is a
tank of stone masonry, a single mass measuring 22 feet
by 7 feet, shaped into a tank for water ; a rectangular
wall encircles the whole group. The date of these
buildings is put by Captain Cole at A.D. 1 ; but the
true date may be some five centuries later, the period
which is sometimes assigned to the buildings at
Martand, Pandritan, and elsewhere.

CHAPTER VII.

ROUTES IN THE VALLEY OF KASHMIR AND TO SPORTING GROUNDS AND TO PLACES BEYOND.

THE following tables of routes are intended for the use of those who may be anxious to visit the sporting grounds in the valley and beyond ; or who may wish to travel in the different places named. Other routes in the valley will be found in previous chapters.

Route 1.—Srinagar to Gilgit.

No.	Stages.		Miles.	Remarks.
	Srinagar to—			
1	Sumbal	...	17	
2	Bandipur	...	18	Usually by boat.
3	Tragbal	...	9	
4	Zotkusu	...	9	Across Rajdiangan pass, 11,800 feet.
5	Kazalwan	...	6	Cross Kishengunga river.
6	Gures	...	11	
7	Gurikot	...	11	Alternative route by Burzil.
8	Kalapani	...	12	Cross Kamri pass, 13,160 feet.
9	Lohinhadar	...	14	
10	Pukarkot	...	10	
11	Chagam	...	12	
12	Gurikot (in Astor)	...	14	A Cantonment.
13	Astor or Hasora	...	7	
14	Harcho	..	11	
15	Mushkim	...	8	
16	Duizan	...	8½	
17	Ramghat	...	12	Cross Hatu pass, 10,000 feet.
18	Bunji	...	6	Here is a bridge across the Indus.
19	Jagrot	...	12	Cross ridge.
20	Camp	...	7	
21	Minawar	...	8	
22	Gilgit	...	11	
	Total	...	333½	

The Gilgit route beyond Gures is closed to visi tors who have not obtained the special sanction of the Resident.

Route 2.—Alternative Route from Gures to Gilgit.

No.	Stages.		Miles.	Remarks.
	Srinagar to			
6	Gures	...	70	
7	Bangla	..	11	
8	Mapanum	...	9	
9	Burzil	..	9	
10	Camp	...	12	Cross Dorkin pass, 13,500 ft.
11	Das	...	9	
12	Gudhai	...	12	
13	Nargam		8	
14	Astor	...	12	
23	Gilgit	...	86½	
	Total	.-	238½	

Route 3.—Srinagar to Leh.

No.	Stages.		Miles.	Remarks.
	Srinagar to			
1	Gandarbal	...	14	
2	Kangan	...	12	
3	Gund	...	14	Beyond this supplies should be carried to Dras.
4				
5	Gagangir	...	9	
6	Sonamarg	...	10	
7	Baltal	...	10	
	Matayan	...	16	Cross Zogi pass, 11,500 ft.
	Dras	...	15	Rest-houses bad after this stage.
8	Tashgam	...	15	
11	Chenagund	...	18	
12	Kargil	...	8	
13	Shargol	...	20	
	Kharbu	...	18	Cross Namika La, 13,000 ft.
14	Lamayuru	...	16	Cross Fotu La, 13,000 feet.
15	Nurulla	..	18	Cross Indus.
16	Saspal	...	17	
17	Ninsu	...	13	
18	Pitak	...	13	
19	Leh	...	5	
	Total	...	250	

A fairly good riding path throughout, except in winter, when the Zoji pass is impracticable.

From Khalsi an alternative route crosses the plateau away from the river.

No.	Stages.	Miles.	Remarks.
15	Lamayuru ...	...	
16	Khalsı ...	12	
17	Timisgam ..	10	
18	Tarutse ...	17	
19	Ninsu	10	Joins usual route.
20	Leh ...	18	
	Total ...	67	

Route 4.—Srinagar to Leh, viâ Wardwan.

No.	Stages.	Miles.	Remarks.
	Srinagar to—		
2	Islamabad ..	35	
3	Karpur ...	13	Cross a low ridge.
4	Gooran ...	14	Passing Naobog.
5	Camp below pass ...	...	Cross Margan pass, 11,600 feet. Difficult in the early summer.
6	Inshin ...	20	
7	Suknes ...	15	The last village of Wardwan valley.
8	Domhoi ...	9	
9	Moskolu ...	12	
10	Camp ...	12	Cross Bhotkol pass, 14,370 feet.
11	Suru ...	10	
12	Sankho ..	18	Follow down Suru river.
13	Camp ...	13	
14	Kargil ...	13	Join route 3.
23	Leh ...	120	
	Total ...	304	

From Suru there is also a nearer path to Shargol—
a rough march of three days over a pass.   This route is
impracticable for horses, excepting in the early summer.
It is at all times difficult.

Route 5.—Srinagar to Kishtwar.

No.	Stages.		Miles.	Remarks.
	Srinagar to			
1	Islamabad	...	35	By land or water.
2	Sagan	...	14	
3	Wankringi	...	12	Huts below the pass.
4	Singhpur	...	16	Across the Mar Bal pass.
5	Mogul Maidan	..	16	Down the Kesbere Khol.
6	Kishtwar	...	10	Cross the Marev, Ardwan, and Chenab rivers by rope bridges.
	Total	...	103	

Route 6.—Srinagar to Skardu, viâ Dras.

No.	Stages.		Miles.	Remarks.
	Srinagar to—			
9	Tashgam	...	115	*Vide* route 3.
10	Karkitchu	...	14	Villages and supplies at each stage.
11	Gangani	...	10	
12	Oltingthang	...	12	Indus runs below this.
13	Tarkuti	...	14	
14	Kartaksho	...	17	Road very bad in summer. Frequent ascents. Path occasionally built on scaffolding.
15	Tolti	...	12	
16	Parkuta	...	14	
17	Gol	...	13	
18	Kepchung	...	17	
19	Skardu	...	4	
	Total	...	242	

The route to Skardu by Desai is only practicable from
the 15th July to the 15th September. The country
from Gilgit to Skardu, Dras and Leh is recommended
to sportsmen. Big-game hunters also visit Chang
chenmo—11 marches, or 122 miles from Leh, over the
Changla pass, 18,000 feet, and the Masse-Mik-La,
18,400 feet. This road never descends below 11,000
feet, and is very often 16,000 feet above sea level.

There are two routes to Simla from Srinagar, one by
Kangra and Chamba, and the other by Kulu, Chamba,
and Bhadrawar, but special passes from the Resident'
are needed before these routes can be used.

Route 7.— Srinagar to Simla, by Kangra and Chamba.

No.	Stages.	Miles.	Remarks.
	Srinagar to—		
1	Islamabad ...	35	By land. Generally by boat.
2	Lukbowa Nag ...	8	
3	Shahabad ...	5	Large village. Supplies plentiful.
4	Vernag ...	4	Baradari. Supplies and coolies abundant.
5	Chaon ...	10	Cross Braribal pass: steep ascent and descent.
6	Camp ...	13	
7	Gayi ...	7	Bad road.
8	Bhagwan ...	9	
9	Dada ..	7	Cross river Chandra Bhaga by rope bridge.
10	Kalen ..	10	
11	Bhadrawar ..	11	Cross Padre pass: short ascent and very steep descent.
12	Camp (Mur) or Bhadrawar to	12	Thannala 8 Langera 15 Thunun 9 Manjeri 12
	Carried over ...	131	

No.	Stages.	Miles.	Remarks.
	Brought forward ...	131	
13	Bungul ...	10	Bad road.
14	Digil or Kirah ..	11	Do.
15	Manjeri ...	11	Steep ascent, cross low pass. Cross river Shool on massaks.
16	Chamba ...	16	Road bad, cross the Ravi by bridge. Baradari.
17	Rareri ...	6	Cross pass, steep ascent for 5 miles.
18	Chuari ...	14	Road bad for ponies.
19	Rapir ...	6	Ditto
20	Sihanta ...	12	Ditto.
21	Rilloo (Hutli) ...	12	
22	Kangra ...	13	Dâk bungalow ; *serai*. Good accommodation may sometimes be had at the Sessions House, if application is made to the Deputy Commissioner of the District.
23	Ranital ..	9	Dâk bungalow.
24	Juala Mukhi ...	12	*Serai.* Many interesting temples : some are in ruins.
25	Nadaon ...	7	Good camping ground on the maidan. The Rajah is very hospitable, often lending his bungalow to visitors.
26	Hamirpur ..	15	Bungalow and thana.
27	Dangah ...	10	
28	Kunar Hati ...	8	Cross Sutlej river by ferry.
29	Belaspur ...	10	
30	Sahiki Hati ...	17	Bungalow.
31	Sairi ..	16	Dâk bungalow.
32	Simla ...	10	
	Total ...	362	

Route 8.—Srinagar to Simla, by Kulu, Chamba and Bhadrawar.

No.	Stages.	Miles.	Remarks.
	Srinagar to—		
21	Rilloo (Hutli) ...	229	See route to Simla by Kangra and Chamba.
22	Bhagsu Cant. ...	17	Cross several torrents, Dharmsala is just above Bhagsu. Encamping ground and dâk bungalow. Dharmsala is a charming little station with many English resi-, dents. There is a church, assembly room, etc.
23	Bundleh ...	19	Putiyar is about half way between Budlah and Bhagsu.
24	Baijnath ...	11	Dâk bungalow and encamping ground.
25	Haurbaug ..	17	} Old route.
26	Fatakal ...	10	
27	Sauri ...	11	Cross river by bridge ; ascent.
28	Komaud ...	8	Cross pass ; steep ascent.
29	Bajaora ..	13	Dâk bungalow. Cross the Bias river below Bajaora, and the Sainij river near Larji.
30	Larji ...	13	Bungalow.
31	Manglaor (Plach) ...	9	Cross the Chata river.
32	Jeebhi or Rasala ...	11	Re-cross the Chata river and cross a large tributary stream.
33	Kot ...	12	Cross the Jalori pass.
34	Dularsh ...	18	Steep ascent ; cross a ridge.
35	Kotgarh ...	14	Cross the river Sutlej by bridge ; very steep descent and ascent.
36	Narkunda ...	12	Bungalow. Or from Kot to Choi 11, Dila 9, Narkunda 17 miles.
37	Matiana ...	13	Dâk bungalow.
38	Theog ...	8	Do.
39	Fagu ...	12	Do
.	Mahasu ...	......	Do. on new road.
40	Simla ...	10	
	Total ...	467	

Route 9.—Srinagar to Dalhousie.

No.	Stages.	Miles.	Remarks.
	Srinagar to—		
	Batoti	......	*Vide* Jammu Road.
	Assar	12	
	Kapeni	12	
	Kuteni	12	
	Bhadrawar	12	
	Thanala	12	
	Langera	6	
	Bhandal	17	
	Manjir	14	
	Chamla	14	
	Kajean	7	
	Dalhousie	9	
	Total	127	

Drew in his book gives 30 different routes to and from various parts of Kashmir. He describes five routes to Yarkand from Leh, two from Palampore and one from Simla. Knight in that capital story of travel, "Where Three Empires Meet," fully describes a journey from "Srinagar to Leh," then to the monastery of Himis, and then to Gilgit, Hunza, and Nagar across Baltistan. Lord Dunmore's book gives an account of his journey to the Pamirs and onward to Central Asia. Neve's little volume should also be consulted regarding unfrequented routes from and to Kashmir. In this book will be found details of the route from Abbottabad to Chilas, *via* Khagan, and also a route to Kashmir from Muzaffarabad, *via* Kishnaganga.

APPENDIX.

I.

COINS, WEIGHTS AND MEASURES.

COINS.

THE Maharajah's coins in circulation in Kashmir are the old *Kham* rupee, equal to 8 annas of the Indian rupee, and the *chilki*—the latest issue of silver coins, and now only issued—equal to 10 annas of the Indian rupee; 8 pieces of copper make up one anna of the Maharajah's coin, equal to 12 pies or 4 pice of the Indian anna. The *Kham* rupee, called the *kohna* or old coin, and the *chilki*, called the *newi* or new coin, are both marked with the letters J. H. S. Some sort of mystery seems to hang over the placing of these letters on the Kashmir coins, and which Englishmen take to be the Christian monogram; but, so far as the unauthenticated history of these coins is concerned, the reason for having these letters on them may be found in the following story.

When Ranjit Singh was ruler of Kashmir, there was a silver coin called Nanak Shah, after the founder of the Seikh religion, and the value of this coin was equal to 16 annas. This was found to be inconveniently large, mainly owing to the slender means of the people amongst whom it circulated. Accordingly the *Kham* rupee, of 8 annas only, was introduced; but before this was done, the Nanak Shah coin had been issued from the Mint, which then existed in Srinagar, of less intrinsic value than formerly, or than it ought to have been. When this was discovered, the Master of the Mint was held to be responsible, and as a punishment, both his ears were cut off. After the annexation of the Punjab, between the years 1853 and 1859, when Sir John Law. rence was Chief Commissioner of the Punjab, in certain negotiations with the Maharajah of Kashmir, Sir John Lawrence made some objections to the silver coins in circulation in His Highness' dominions. In order to conform to the Chief Commissioner's wishes for some change, the three letters J. H. S. were stamped on the coins. The meaning of this monogram may be, there. fore, the representation of the three words Jammu, Highness, Singh ; or, more fully, His Highness (Golab) Singh. Sir John Lawrence was pleased with this, and His Highness was equally gratified, and thus the wishes of two important persons were complied with.

The Indian rupee and the smaller silver coins and copper money are commonly used in preference to the Maharajah's coins. Government of India currency notes and bank cheques are easily cashed during the season.

WEIGHTS.

The following weights are in common use in Kashmir :—

1   Kham rupee = nearly 1 tola of 10½ Mashas. (In British India 1 tola = 12 Mashas.) The Masha = 15 grains troy.

4⅜ Kham rupees = 1 Chatak.

4   Chataks   = 1 Pauwa or 9 Kham rupees.

4   Pauwas   = 1 Seer   or 76 Kham rupees.

6   Seers   = 1 Trák of 486 Kham rupees.

16 Tráks   = 1 Kharwar.

With the Government of Kashmir 15 Traks are equal to 1 Kharwar. Shali and produce taken in payment of revenue are paid at this rate. The *man*, which in the Punjab is 40 seers, is in Kashmir 45 seers, and the Kashmir Kharwar is equal to 2 *mans* of 45 seers each.

MEASURES.

Woollen and other goods sold to visitors are measured by the English yard of 36 inches, but the Kashmir yard contains 41 inches. The *girah* or *girih*, frequently mentioned by dealers, is made up of three finger breadths, and 18 *girahs* are equal to 1 *gaz* or yard. In British India 16 *girahs* make 1 *gaz*, and is equal to 2¼ inches. In Kashmir it is equal to 2⅝ inches.

II.

List of Post and Telegraph Offices in Kashmir and Jammu.

POST OFFICES.

In Kashmir—	In Jammu—
Srinagar.	Jammu.
Bargam.	Aknur.
Bijbehara.	Arnia.
Dras.	Basoli
Magam	Chomak.
Mulshabag.	Dansal.
Nehalpore.	Homerpur Sidhar.
Palwama.	Kahna Chak.
Sonamarg.	Mirpore.
Avantipore.	Munwar.
Gures.	Ramgarh.
Minimarg.	Ranbir Singhpore.

Bandipore.
Baramulla.
Handwara.
Sopore.
Gulmarg.
Islamabad.
Kullgam.
Shupyan
Vernag.
Kargil.
Leh.
Skardu.
Chakoti.
Domel.
Garhi.
Hattian.
Muzuffnalas.
Rampor.
Uri
Karnah.

Satwari.
Tawi.
Bhimber.
Katna.
Jasrota.
Prol.
Naushera.
Kotli.
Prat.
Rajaun.
Serai.
Thana.
Saula.
Jasmergarh.
Udampore.
Banhal.
Batout.
Bhadrawar.
Paddar.
Ramluri.
Ramnagur.
Reasi.

IMPERIAL TELEGRAPH OFFICES.

Gilgit.
Bunji.
Chilas.
Astor.
Minimarg.
Gures.
Bandipore.

Srinagar.
Sopore.
Baramulla.
Rampor.
Uri.
Garhi.
Domel.

STATE TELEGRAPH OFFICES.

Sonamarg.
Dras.
Kargil.
Skardu.
Islamabad.
Vernag.
Banhal.

Ramban.
Udairpore.
Botul.
Jammu.
Naushera.
Tawi

III.

GAME LAWS FOR LADAKH, SKARDU, AND BALTISTAN.

It has been observed that the coolies and shikaris of Kashmir engaged by European visitors and taken up to Skardu and Ladakh often use violence to the people and create trouble by non-payment for the supplies and carriage obtained from the villagers. In the hope of preventing complaints arising from this cause, the following rules have been framed and passed by the State Council :—

(I) The local officers shall open a register of all' *shikaris* residing in Ladakh who are known to be competent and willing to accompany visitors in search of game. Many excellent men are to be found among the Ladakhis, and gentlemen desirous of shooting in Ladakh are advised, if possible, to employ Ladakhi *shikaris*, in place of men from Kashmir.

(II) To facilitate the engagement of Ladakhi *shikaris*, copies of the register referred to in rule (I) will be supplied to and circulated among visitors in Srinagar by Babu Amar Nath, who will be able to give the necessary information as to where, and how, any *shikari* selected for employment can be engaged.

(III) Officers who nevertheless wish to employ Kashmiri *shikaris* in Ladakh should, before starting, register, with the Assistant Resident in Kashmir, Srinagar, the names of their *shikari* and of his *chota shikari*, stating also the *shikaris'* fathers' names, residence and the district, and, if possible, the *nullah* in which it is proposed to shoot. This information is necessary in order that the names of Kashmiri *shikaris*, going to Ladakh, may be known and notice taken of misconduct.

(IV) Copies of the register kept by the Assistant
Resident in Kashmir under rule (III) will be sent to
the Assistant Resident for Leh and to the Governor in
Kashmir, and in the event of any misconduct being
proved against any *shikari* permitted to go to Ladakh,
his name will be noted and permission to go to Ladakh
in future will be withheld.

(V) In order to prevent inconvenience to officers
wishing to travel to Ladakh direct from Baramulla, the
information required by rule (III) may be given to the
Assistant Resident by letter, or *shikaris* who have been
actually engaged beforehand, by officers in India, may
themselves register their names with the Assistant
Resident in Srinagar before joining their employers.
It should be clearly understood that any Kashmiri
shikari employed in Ladakh, whose name has not been
registered, will be liable to the punishment mentioned
in rule (IV).

(Sd.) H. S. BARNES,
Resident in Kashmir.

KASHMIR RESIDENCY :
Dated Sialkot, the 10th March, 1895.

IV.

TAX ON BOATS.

An annual tax is levied on all boats owned and employed in the valley of Kashmir, according to the follow-

ing schedule ; the tax is payable by the owner and not by the occupier of the boat.

	Rs.	A.	P
House boat, 1st class	7	0	0
Do.　　2nd class	5	(	
Do.　　3rd class		c	
Doonga or large Kashmiri living boat, 1st class　..		0	0
Do.　　do.　　2nd class		0	0
Do.　　do.　　3rd class		4	0
Do.　　do.　　4th class		0	0
Shikari or small Kashmiri boat, per shikari		8	(
Boats used for shali, bhoosa and wood, 1st class　.		0	0
Do.　　do.　　2nd class　..		0	0
Khachu boats used for stones, lime, earth, &c.	1	0	0

V.

RULES FOR TRADERS IN KASHMIR.

(1). No trader shall attempt to approach or enter into a boat occupied by a visitor while the boat is passing on the river.

(2). Nor shall he enter into a boat, or tent or house occupied by a visitor without permission obtained by sending his card. If told to do so, he must leave the place at once.

(3). No hawking is allowed in places other than those appointed.

(4). Traders should not send their cards immediately on arrival of a visitor, nor should they molest visitors when they are at meals or otherwise engaged.

(5) Making noise is not allowed near tents, houses or boats occupied by visitors.

(6). If prohibited by a police constable or a servant, no trader shall go close to a tent or boat or house occupied by a visitor.

VI.

Rules for Observance by Visitors and Residents in the Territories of H. H. the Maharajah of Jammu and Kashmir.

GOVERNMENT OF INDIA.
FOREIGN DEPARTMENT.
NOTIFICATION.
No. 85 E.

FORT WILLIAM, *the 13th January*, 1888.

In supersession of the Notification of the Government of India in the Foreign

* NOTE.—Copies of these Rules can be obtained from the Resident in Kashmir.

Department, No. 679 F., dated the 28th April, 1885, the following revised Rules,* for observance by all Europeans, Americans and Australians, who are now, or may be hereafter, in the territory of His Highness the Maharajah of Jammu and Kashmir, which have been drawn up with the consent of His Highness the Maharajah, and have received the sanction of the Governor-General in Council, are published for information :—

I.—(1) Military or Civil Officers of the British Government may, at any time, and without passes, visit and reside in the territories of His Highness the Maharajah of Jammu and Kashmir,

†At present there is no limit.

subject to such limit† in number as the Government of India, with the concurrence of His Highness the Maharajah, may prescribe, and subject also, in the case of Military Officers, to the military regulations or orders for the time being in force.

(2) Other Europeans, Americans or Australians, wishing to visit or reside in the said territories, require passes, which may be granted (in the Form A annexed) by the Resident in Kashmir.

II.—Information as to the usual routes for entering and leaving Kashmir may be obtained from the Assistant Resident. The route *viâ* Jammu and Banhal is private, and may not be used except with the special permission of His Highness the Maharajah obtained through the Resident.

III.—Persons subject to these rules are not allowed to travel from Kashmir to Simla (or *vice versâ*) across the hills, or the plains (or *vice versâ*), *viâ* Kishtwar, Bhadrawar and Chamba, except with the special permission of His Highness the Maharajah obtained through the Resident.

IV.—No request should be preferred to the ordinary officials of His Highness the Maharajah, except in real emergencies. An officer of the Darbar is appointed by His Highness the Maharajah to attend to the wants of the European community at Srinagar, and application may be made to him for assistance in petty matters. All payments must be made at the rates demanded, which, if deemed exorbitant, can be reported to the Resident in Kashmir.

V.—Complaints should be preferred, with statements of the circumstances, to the Resident in Kashmir.

VI.—No present may be accepted from His Highness the Maharajah or his officers.

VII.—Persons subject to these rules, who may be desirous of paying their respects to His Highness the Maharajah, can be introduced by the Resident on suitable occasions ; and all arrangements for official visits to Jammu or Srinagar should be made through the Resident.

VIII.—The customs and regulations of His Highness the Maharajah's Territory should be carefully observed by persons subject to these rules, and by their servants.

IX.—When attending evening entertainments given by His Highness the Maharajah, Military Officers should wear, subject to the military regulations or orders for the time being in force, either uniform or evening dress, and other visitors or residents should wear evening dress.

X.—The Resident may, from time to time, with the concurrence of His Highness the Maharajah, prescribe limits of travel, beyond which no one will be allowed to go, unless supplied with a special pass obtained from the Resident.

XI.—Rules may, from time to time, be made by the Resident, with the concurrence of His Highness the Maharajah, regarding the routes for entering, leaving and travelling in Kashmir, the rates to be paid for coolies, transport, supplies and other minor matters.

XII.—The Resident in Kashmir is authorised to require any person subject to these rules, who breaks any of them, to leave the territories of His Highness the Maharajah of Jammu and Kashmir. If any such requisitions on the part of the Resident is not at once complied with, the matter will be reported by him for the orders of the Governor-General in Council.

Form A.

Pass No. of 189

of is permitted to travel ⎰ in the territories
or reside ⎱ of His Highness

the Maharajah of Jammu and Kashmir from the
to the   189 , subject to the conditions noted on
the back of this pass.

This pass may be cancelled or withdrawn at any
time, and it requires renewal at the end of the period
for which it is current.

Endorsement on Reverse of Pass.

I agree to conform to the rules prescribed by the
Government of India for observance by Europeans,
Americans and Australians in the territories of His
Highness the Maharajah of Jammu and Kashmir.
I will return this pass to the Office of the Resident in
Kashmir at the end of the period for which it is
current.

General Rules.

1. All visitors to Srinagar are requested to communicate their names and dates of arrival to the Darbar
official deputed to attend on European visitors. The
official for the time being is Rai Sahib Amar Nath.

2. Visitors are advised, in their own interests, to
procure such Kashmiri servants as they may require,
specially boatmen and *shikaris*, through Rai Sahib
Amar Nath, and not through local bankers.

3. Visitors to Srinagar are not permitted to encamp
in the Dilawar Khan Bagh situated within the city, nor
in the Nishat, Shalimar or Chashmah Shahi gardens on
the Dal Lake. The fixed camping places are the
Munshi, Hari Singh, Ram Munshi and Chinar Baghs
at Srinagar, and the Nasim Bagh on the Dal lake.
Visitors are also informed that the plot of ground at

Sumbal, known as the " Nandi Keshwar Bhairava," should not be used for camping purposes.

4. Visitors wishing to visit the Fort or Palace at Srinagar are required to give at least one full day's notice of their intention to the Rai Sahib deputed to attend on European visitors.

5. Cows and bullocks are, under no circumstances, to be slain in the territories of His Highness the Maharajah, and visitors are requested to take precautions that their dogs do not worry these animals.

6. Visitors about to proceed into the interior and wishing to be supplied with carriage, are requested to communicate with the Rai Sahib, at least 30 hours before the time fixed for their departure. Failing this notice, the Rai Sahib cannot be responsible for the supply of carriage in proper time.

7. Travellers in the interior should not encamp within villages. They are advised to encamp only at the ordinary stages and camping-grounds; supplies are not usually available in any other place.

8. Persons going on shooting excursions are required to take carriage and supplies with them. They may not demand them in places where no provision is made for supplying them, and they are forbidden to press into their service the people of the country as beaters for game.

9. Visitors to the Skardu district are informed that the route, via the Deosai plains, from Skardu to Bandipore, is reserved, and passes to use the same will only be issued to a few visitors by the Kashmir Darbar through the Residency, and under the conditions that those, to whom such passes are given, will be prepared

to pay double the rates for carriage and coolie transport now in force on that route in cases in which it is necessary to make local arrangements for transport and supplies. Visitors are also informed that when visiting the Skardu district, they should make their own arrangements for transport, as the local officials of the Kashmir Darbar will not be bound to meet their requisitions for transport.

9 (a). Visitors are also informed that no supplies, except wood and grass, are obtainable, nor should they be requisitioned at the village of Tolti in the Skardu district on the Dras-Skardu route.

10. Visitors are not permitted to shoot in the tract of country extending along the lake from the Tukht-i-Suleiman to the Shalimar gardens, or anywhere in the hills between the Sindh and Lidar rivers, or in the Wangat valley, or any *nullah* thereof, all which are preserves of His Highness the M a h a rajah. Shooting on the tracts marginally noted, which are private property, is also prohibited; and no one should shoot anywhere in Jammu territory without a *parwána* obtained from the Darbar through the Resident.

Dopatta, Kukiawála, Machipura, Danuachikar, Uri, Banyar and in the territory of the Rajah of Kharmong in Baltistan without the permission of the Rajah.

The attention of sportsmen is invited to notifications issued by the State Council for the preservation of game in Kashmir published at pages 177 to 179 of this book.

11. Visitors are prohibited from shooting heron in Kashmir.

12. Fishing is prohibited at the places marginally noted, as also between the first and third bridge in Srinagar and in the Jammu Province, unless a *parwána* has been previously obtained from the Darbar through the Resident.

Martund, Vernag, Anantnag, Devi Khirbhowani.

13. Visitors are not allowed to encamp in the gardens and pavilion at Achhabal, which are the private property of His Highness the Maharajah, nor are their servants allowed to make cooking-places there.

14. When the Dal gate is closed, no attempt should be made to remove the barrier or to lift boats over the bund to or from the lake.

15. Application for houses or for quarters in the barracks at Srinagar should be made to the State Engineer, Kashmir Darbar, Srinagar.

16. A visitor may not sub-let his house or quarters, and no visitor may rent more than one set of quarters, except with special permission.

17. Rent must be paid on demand, or in advance, when required, to the State Engineer, Kashmir Darbar.

18. When attending evening entertainments given by His Highness the Maharajah in honor of Her Majesty the Queen-Empress, Military Officers should appear in Mess uniform.

19. Visitors are particularly requested to be careful that their servants do not import into the valley articles for sale, on which duty is leviable. The baggage of visitors is not examined by the Maharajah's Customs officials, and, in return for this courtesy, it is expected that any evasion of the Customs Regulations will be discountenanced.

Subject to this provision, and with effect from 11th April, 1897, Customs duty according to the tariff in force in the State will be charged on all goods imported by both visitors to, and residents in Kashmir.

20. Servants of visitors found in the city after dark, and any servant found without a light after the evening gun has fired, will be liable to be apprehended by the police.

21. Servants of visitors found resorting for purposes of nature to places other than the fixed latrines are liable to punishment.

22. Grass-cutters are prohibited from cutting grass in, or in the neighbourhood of, the gardens occupied by European visitors.

23. All persons are required to settle all accounts before they leave Kashmir, and are responsible that the debts of their servants are similarly discharged.

24. Complaints of the nature of civil suits against subjects of His Highness the Maharajah can only be taken cognizance of by the State Courts, and against all British Indian subjects who are visitors to Kashmir, by the Court of the Assistant Resident on payment of the usual Court fees.

25. Visitors are reminded that the forests in the Jammu and Kashmir State are in charge of the State Forest Department, and that no trees may be felled without permission, and payment of the price.

Application for trees and for permission to cut them should be made to the Conservator of Forests, Srinagar, or to the nearest Forester.

26. A dairy has been established, under State supervision, behind Doctor Neve's Hospital. Milk can be obtained there twice a day at the rates in the

" Nirakhnámah," which is posted at the Library, or is obtainable from Rai Sahib Amar Nath, the Darbar official deputed to attend on visitors.

Visitors should send their own cans for milk, and they are reminded that the Kashmiri seer is less by about 2 chittacks than the Indian seer.

27. Visitors to Gulmarg are requested to kindly warn their grass-cutters not to encroach on the cultivated parts of villages.

Grass can always be cut from the Tang Marg.

28. The attention of visitors is called to the special notices printed at pages 196 to 205.

JAMMU.

29. Visitors to Jammu are informed that permission to visit the town and to occupy rooms in the State Travellers' Bungalow must be obtained from the Assistant Resident in Kashmir, who will issue passes to approved persons on receipt of application.

This rule does not apply to Officers of Her Majesty's Service in Civil and Military employment.

30. These rules will be revised and new rules added, from time to time, as circumstances may require. Any doubt as to the meaning of any rule will be decided by the Resident.

NOTIFICATION.

No. 232, *dated* 21*st April,* 1896.

GAME LAWS OF JAMMU AND KASHMIR STATE.

The following rules for the preservation of game are published for general information :—

1. Driving game with men and dogs in Kashmir, including Gilgit, Ladakh and Skardu, is prohibited,

except in the case of Bears, Leopards and Pigs, driving and beating for which is allowed between 15th May and 15th October, but not at other times of the year. The destruction of all females of the following animals : Barasingha, Ovis Ammon, Yak, Shahpoo, (Oorial) or Burhel, Markhor, Ibex, Thibetan Antelope, Thibetan Ravine Deer, and Serow, is absolutely prohibited in Kashmir. No Musk Deer, either male or female, are to be shot or taken.

2. The sale in Kashmir of the horne and skins of any of the animals mentioned in Rule 1, excepting the skins of Bears and Leopards, is prohibited.

3. The breeding season of Pheasant, Chikor, and Partridge extends from 15th March to 15th September, inclusive, in each year.

During the breeding season, as above defined, the shooting of any of the birds above-mentioned, their destruction by nets or in any other fashion, or the taking of their eggs, is absolutely prohibited. During the breeding season no person shall sell in Kashmir any such bird recently killed or taken.

4. During the shooting season, *i.e.*, from 16th September to 14th March, the netting, trapping and ensnaring of the above-mentioned birds is also probibited.

5. Whoever intentionally commits a breach of Rules 1 and 2 shall be punished on first conviction by a fine not exceeding Rs. 25, or with imprisonment for a term not exceeding one month, or both; and on second conviction, by a fine not exceeding Rs. 100, or with imprisonment not exceeding four months, or both, together with forfeiture of the guns or other weapons

and dogs of the offender to the State, and if the offender is a *shikari*, with forfeiture of license for one year; provided that, when the offender is a European, or the servant of a European, the case shall be immediately reported to the Resident for disposal in such manner as he may think fit.

6. Subject to the same proviso, any person convicted of a breach of Rules 3 and 4 shall be punished by a fine not exceeding in each case Rs. 25.

7. His Highness the Maharajah may, by order in writing, relax any or all of the foregoing rules in favour of any person.

AMAR SINGH, RAJA,
Vice-President of the Jammu and Kashmir
State Council.

Countersigned—
A. C. TALBOT,
Resident in Kashmir.

PUBLIC WORKS DEPARTMENT.
Jammu and Kashmir State.

Rules for Rental of Huts at Gulmarg sanctioned by the State Council, under Resolution No. 22, dated 8th October, 1896.

The huts in Schedule A are available for rental on the following conditions :—

1. No hut will be allotted until the full season's rent has been deposited with the State Engineer, and priority of deposits shall constitute priority of claim to allotment.

2. Such deposit will be refunded in event of failure to occupy, subject to the following deductions :—

A deduction of Rs. 10, if notification of relinquishment is given before 1st April.

A deduction of Rs. 20, if such notice is given after
1st April and before 1st June.

One-half the deposit will be forfeited, if such notice
is not given until after June 1st.

3. Tenants may dispose of their right of occupancy
for any period of a season for which they shall have
paid the full rent in advance, provided that, in each
case, the terms of the arrangement shall be clearly defined in a written agreement (signed by both parties
thereto), and that a copy thereof shall be filed in the
Office of the State Engineer for record and for reference
of the Resident in case of disputes arising.

4. It is to be clearly understood that the foregoing
rule is framed solely for the convenience of tenants who
may be unable to occupy their premises after allotment
for part or whole of the season; it is not intended to
permit of the acquirement and sub-letting of the huts
for purposes of profit, which is prohibited.

5. The payment of rent as fixed will entitle the
tenant to the use of the premises as detailed in the schedule, in a state of reasonable and water-tight repair,
but the tenant will be liable for all breakages which
may occur during his tenancy.

6. Any tenant wishing to add to the accommodation
of his holding may do so, with the previous sanction of
the State Engineer, at his own cost, and on the understanding that such additions become the absolute property of the State.

7. Any tenant adding to his holding under the
foregoing rule shall have the right to occupy the
same without enhancement of rent for as many
consecutive seasons as he wishes, provided that

he shall pay the full season's rent in advance on demand.

The huts in schedule B are available for allotment on the following conditions :—

8. No hut will be allotted until the nominal ground-rental of Rs. 20 for the season has been deposited with the State Engineer.

9. Tenants may occupy and add in any way they choose to the existing premises, subject to the provisions of rules 3, 4, 6 and 7, but the State will be in no way responsible for repairs or up-keep.

10. Any person wishing to build on a new site may do so free of charge for the first year, provided that the Resident's approval of the site has been first obtained, and also provided that, after the first year, the premises shall become subject to rules 8 and 9.

11. Tenants (Schedule A) asking P.'W. D. to make additions or changes, or tenants (Schedule B) asking for repairs to their huts, will be charged 10 per cent. commission on the amount of expenditure.

M. NETHERSOLE, c.e.,
STATE ENGINEER,
Jammu and Kashmir State.

AMAR SINGH, RAJA,
Vice-President of State Council·

SCHEDULE A.
Gulmarg Huts for Rental.

Hut No. 1.—A new 4-roomed hut, 2 bath-rooms, 1 small godown, no pantry, stone nogging walls, shingle roof, 1 kitchen, 4 servants' quarters, 6 stables, plank walls, and plank and shingle roof: rent Rs. 130 per season.

Hut No. 2.—A new 8-roomed hut, 4 bath-rooms, 1 store-room and 1 pantry, stone nogging walls, shingle roof, with 1 kitchen, 3 stables and 3 servants' quarters, all shingled: rent Rs. 200 per season.

Hut No. 4.—New, 3 rooms, 2 bath-rooms, 1 pantry, plank wall, shingle roof, kitchen, servants' quarters 3, stables 3, verandah in front of stables, plank wall and shingle roof: rent Rs. 130 per season.

Hut No. 5.—New, same as hut No. 4: rent Rs. 130 per season.

Hut No. 7.—New, 4 rooms, 3 bath-rooms, 1 pantry, 1 kitchen, plank walls, shingle roof, 6 servants' quarters, plank wall, shingle roof, stables 5, old pacherbandi wall, mud roof, 2 old pacherbandi servants' quarters: rent Rs. 130 per season.

Hut No. 8.—Dining-room and drawing-room, mud roof, 4 large bed-rooms, shingle roof, 4 bath-rooms, pantry and 3 godowns, 6 servants' houses, 8 stables: rent Rs 270 per season.

Hut No. 10.—New, 3 rooms, 2 bath-rooms, 1 pantry, nogging walls, shingle roof, with 1 new hut close by, with 1 room, 1 bath room, plank wall, shingle roof, 1 new kitchen, 4 new servants' quarters weather boarded walls and shingle roofs, 4 stables, pacherbandi walls, and shingle roof: rent Rs. 130 per season

Hut No. 22*A*.—New, 4 rooms, 2 bath-rooms, no pantry, weather boarded walls and shingle roof, 3 servants' houses, shingle roof: rent Rs. 80 per season.

Hut No. 22*B*.—Old, 3 rooms, 2 bath-rooms, pacherbandi walls, mud roof, 1 new hut close by, 3 rooms,

2 bath-rooms, weather boarded walls, shingle roof, 1 kitchen with the old hut, 4 weather boarded servants' quarters, new shingle roof: rent Rs. 130 per season.

Hut No. 25.—New, 4 rooms, 2 bath-rooms, 1 pantry, nogging walls, shingle roof, 1 kitchen, new, and 4 servants' quarters, weather boarded, shingle roof: rent Rs. 130 per season.

Hut No. 35.—New, 4 rooms, 2 bath-rooms, 1 pantry, nogging walls, shingle roof, 4 new servants' quarters, shingle roof, 1 kitchen, old, pacherbandi walls, mud roof, weather boarded, no stables: rent Rs. 130 per season.

Hut No. 36.—New, 2 rooms, 1 bath-room, verandah, converted into a room, nogging wall, shingle roof, 1 new kitchen, 4 servants' quarters, weather boarded, shingle roof: rent Rs. 70 per season.

Hut No. 24.—New hut, plank walls, shingle roof, 3 living rooms, 2 small dressing-rooms, 4 bath-rooms, pantry and store-rooms, 1 kitchen, 3 servants' quarters, 3 stables, all shingled : rent Rs. 160 per season.

SCHEDULE B.

Old Huts for allotment on payment of ground-rent Rs. 20 per season.

Hut No. 23.—Old, 3 rooms, 2 bath-rooms, 1 pantry, pacherbandi walls, mud roof, 1 new kitchen, 4 new servants' quarters, weather boarded, 1 stable.

Hut No. 26.—Old, 1 room new, with pacherbandi walls, shingle roof, 2 rooms old, pacherbandi walls, mud roof, 2 bath-rooms, 1 pantry, 1 kitchen, 3 servants' quarters, pacherbandi walls, plank roof, sheds for stables.

Hut No. 27.—Old, 3 rooms, 2 bath-rooms, pacherbandi walls, mud roof, 1 kitchen, 3 servants' quarters.

Hut No. 30.—Old, 4 rooms, 3 bath-rooms, pacherbandi walls, mud roof, 2 kitchens, 5 servants' quarters, 2 stables.

Hut No. 31.—Old, 2 rooms, 1 bath-room, pacherbandi walls, mud roof, 1 kitchen, 3 servants' quarters, old, pacherbandi walls, mud roof.

Hut No. 34.—Old, 3 rooms, 3 bath-rooms, 1 pantry, pacherbandi walls, mud roof, 1 new kitchen, 4 servants' quarters, weather boarded, 3 old stables and 4 servants' quarters, pacherbandi walls, mud roof.

Huts Nos. 37 *and* 38.—Old, each with 2 rooms, 1 bath-room, mud roof, no servants' quarters, only 2 kitchens, 4 old stables, pacherbandi walls, mud roof.

Hut No. 39.—Old, 2 rooms, 1 bath-room, 1 pantry, pacherbandi walls, mud roof, very old, 1 new kitchen and 1 new servants' quarters, weather boarded.

Hut No. 40.—Three old rooms, with 1 new kitchen, 3 servants' quarters

LIMITS OF TRAVEL.

Gurais has been fixed as the limit of travel in the Gilgit direction, and the frontier of His Highness' territories in the Ladakh direction. No visitor will be permitted to cross any frontier of Kashmir territory except when contiguous with British India, without a special permit from the Government of India.

TARIFF OF BOAT HIRE IN KASHMIR.

1. Boats hired by the month
    (*a*). Living Boat (Doonga) with crew consisting of at least 4 persons, Rs. 20.
    (*b*). Kitchen Boat (Doonga) with crew consisting of at least 3 persons, Rs. 15.

(c).   Third class Boats (small Doonga) with crew
       consisting of at least 2 persons, Rs. 10.

(d).   Small Boat (*Shikara*), for boat only, Re. 1.
       For each member of the crew of the same,
       Rs. 4 a month in Srinagar.

NOTE,—Women and children over twelve years of age are counted as members of
the crew in the cases of (a), (b) and (c).

The boats belonging to classes (a), (b) and (c) are marked
with a brand L. B., K. B., and 3rd class, respectively.

2.   Wages for extra boatmen employed are annas 4
for each man per diem.

3.   In addition to the rates given above, *rasad* at the
rate of Re. 1 per head per mensem, can be claimed by
every member of the crew when the boats on which
they are employed are taken out of Srinagar.

4.   Boat-hire by distance.

(*i*).   For each member of the crew :—

	Boats of class				
	(a)			(b)	
	Rs	A.	P.	Rs	A.	P.
From Baramulla to Srinagar...	0	10	0	0	8	0
„ Srinagar to Baramulla ..	0	8	0	0	6	0
„ „ „ Islamabad ..	0	10	0	0	8	0
„ „ „ Avantipore	0	6	0	0	5	0
„ Islamabad to Srinagar...	0	8	0	0	6	0
„ Avantipore to Srinagar	0	5	0	0	4	0

(*ii*).   For the trip, crew to consist of the minimum
         laid down in para. (1) :—

	Rs.	A.	P.	Rs.	A.	P.
From Srinagar to Ganderbal	1	4	0	1	2	0
„ „ Awatkala...	3	2	0	3	0	0
„ „ Bandipore	2	0	0	1	12	0

5. When boats are ordered from Srinagar to meet a visitor at any place, half hire of the boat from Srinagar to that place is payable, in addition to the fare due for the journey to the place where the visitor is proceeding.

6. When a boat is not used on the date for which it is ordered, the following rates for each day during which the boat is detained and not used, are payable for detention :—

Class (*a*) annas o 10 o per diem.
  „   (*b*)   „   o 8 o   „
  „   (*c*)   „   o 6 o   „

7. Visitors requiring boats and extra boatmen at Srinagar must apply to **Rai Sahib Amar Nath**, giving 30 hours' notice for the former and 48 for the latter ; and when extra boatmen are required at Sopor to cross the Wular lake on the journey from Baramulla to Srinagar, at least 24 hours' notice must be given to the *Tahsildar* at Sopor.

8. Extra boatmen can only be supplied at the following places on the river, *viz.* :—Baramulla, Sopor, Hajan, Srinagar and Khanabal (Islamabad). They are not procurable at Sumbal, Shadipore, Pampor or Avantipore, the inhabitants of which places are not boatmen by profession, but *zamindars*. In every case at least 24 hours' notice must be given to the Civil authorities for their supply.

9. Visitors are particularly requested to satisfy themselves that the wages of any extra boatmen supplied to them have been properly paid before they are dismissed.

It is also requested that they will be careful to see that firewood, milk and other supplies along the river are regularly paid for by their servants and boatmen.

TARIFF OF HIRE OF COOLIES, PONIES, &c.

1. In all localities in the territories of His Highness the Maharajah of Jammu and Kashmir the standard rate shall be paid for the hire of coolies, &c., except where otherwise specially provided.

2. The standard rate in the said territories is as follows:—

For a coolie carrying the established load of 25 sérs or less ...	4 annas	per stage.
,, coolie carrying a load in excess of 25 sérs but not exceeding 1 maund	6 ,,	,,
,, kahar ...	7 ,,	,,
,, riding pony with English pattern saddle and bridle	1 rupee	,,
,, baggage and servants' pony or mule	8 annas	,,
,, bullocks ...	8 ,,	,,

The load of a baggage pony or mule is 80 sérs; of a *yak* or bullock 60 sérs. Travellers must provide, at their own cost, all ropes required for securing their baggage.

3. The following rates are prescribed for the under-mentioned marches, in supersession of the standard rate :—

THE LADAKH ROAD.

All visitors to Ladakh are required to enter their names, destination and permanent address in the Visitors' List.

The rates for the different marches are as follows :—

	Coolies. Annas.	Ponies. Annas.
Srinagar to Ganderbal or *vice versâ*	4	8
Ganderbal to Kangan	4	8
Kangan to Goond	4	8
Goond to Sonamarg	4	8
Sonamarg to Baltal	4	8
Baltal to Matiun	6	12
Matiun to Dras	4	8
Dras to Tashgam	4	8
Tashgam to Kargil	6	12
Kargil to Shergol	6	12
Shergol to Kharbu	6	12
Kharbu to Lamayuru	4	8
Lamayuru to Nurla	6	12
Nurla to Saspul	4	8
Saspul to Nimo	4	8
Nimo to Phiang or Spitak ,,	4	8
Phiang or Spitak to Leh ,,	2	4

The above rates are not applicable when the passes
are closed by snow

Sportsmen and others wishing to cross the Zojila
pass before the 1st of May will be required to obtain a
parwana from the Assistant Resident for Leh, who
resides at Srinagar, or, in his absence, from the Governor of Kashmir, and who will make the necessary
arrangements for transport, &c.

The rates to be paid to coolies between Goond and
Dras will be entered on the back of the *parwana* in
English and Vernacular, and will vary according to

the season. The maximum being limited to Rs. 5 per coolie.

Sportsmen will not be allowed to cross the pass more than two at a time and at fixed intervals, according to priority of application at Srinagar.

Supplies and transport are obtainable at all the regular stages above, except Matayun, where nothing can be demanded; travellers halting at stages other than those above must take their chance about supplies and not ask to change transport.

Notices to this effect will be found along the whole line.

At Leh there is a furnished dâk bungalow, and all information about the districts beyond Leh is obtainable through the *Waziy* of Ladakh and from the notices in the bungalow.

II.—THE BHIMBER ROUTE.

From Bhimber to Uri 6 annas each coolie and 8 annas each kahar per stage.

From Bhimber to Shupyan 6 annas each coolie and 8 annas each kahar per stage.

The rest-houses on this route are not kept up, and the supply of coolies is limited, and cannot be guaranteed.

III.—THE JHELUM VALLEY CART ROAD.

1. Any traveller may bring his own transport, and is entitled to buy supplies at any dâk bungalow at the prescribed rates on this road.

2. The Darbar cannot guarantee the supply of riding ponies, baggage animals, or coolies along any portion of the road opened to wheeled traffic.

IMPERIAL CARRYING COMPANY,
DHANJIBHOY & SON.

MURREE SECTION.

FROM RAWALPINDI TO MURREE AND *vice versa.*

RATES.

	Rs.	A.	P.
Single Journey by Mail *Tonga*, exclusive of toll ...	8	0	0
Return Journey by Mail *Tonga*, ditto	12	(	
Express *Tonga*, 3 passengers, ditto	24	(	
,, Family *Tonga*, 3 adults and 2 children ...	30	0	0
Bullock Train Carts ...	16	0	(
Packages, not including Glass, Crockery, Furniture and Millinery or other bulky goods, per maund ...			
Glass, Crockery, Furniture and other bulky goods, per maund			
Packages for balf-a-maund or fraction of half-a-maund	0		(
Parcels by *Tonga*, per maund	4		(
Ice Baskets per *Tonga*, under (10 seers)	1		(
Empty Basket	0		(
Ekka, if obtainable	5	8	(
Tongas or carts if brought to private residences to be loaded or unloaded... ...			

KASHMIR SECTION.

FROM MURREE TO SRINAGAR AND *vice versa.*

RATES.

	Rs.	A.	P.
Single Journey by Mail *Tonga* to Baramulla, exclusive of toll	30	(	
Special *Tonga*, 3 passengers, to Baramulla, exclusive of toll ..	00	0	0 (

	Rs.	a.	p.
Special Family *Tonga*, 3 adults and 2 children, to Baramulla, exclusive of toll	120	0	0
Phæton, if available, 3 passengers and 12 seers luggage, to Baramulla	150	c	
Single Journey by Mail *Tonga* to Srinagar, exclusive of toll.	37	c	
Special *Tonga*, 3 passengers, to Srinagar exclusive of toll	110	c	
Special Family *Tonga*, if available, 3 adults and 2 children, to Srinagar, exclusive of toll ...	145	0	0
Phæton, if available, 3 passengers and 12 seers luggage, to Srinagar, exclusive of toll	175	0	0
Bullock Train Carts, to carry not more than 15 maunds, to Baramulla ...	50	0	0
Bullock Train Carts to carry not more than 15 maunds, to Srinagar ...	60	c	
Packages, not including Glass, Crockery, Furniture, Millinery or other bulky goods, to Baramulla, per maund ...	3	8	c
Packages, not including Glass, Crockery, Furniture, Millinery or other bulky goods, to Baramulla, for half or fraction of a half maund ...	1	12	0
Glass, Crockery, Furniture or other bulky goods, per maund	8	c	
Packages from Baramulla to Kashmir, per maund, or fraction thereof	0	8	c
Parcels by *Tonga*, for every 5 seers or fraction of 5 seers ...	1	8	c
Ekkas supplied only by Darbar Chaudri or *Tahsildar*, from Srinagar to Murree ...	18	0	0

Tongas and carts if brought to private residences to be loaded or unloaded

RULES, MURREE SECTION.

I.—*Tongas* are only allowed to run by daylight, except *tongas* carrying the mails between Rawalpindi and Murree and *vice versâ*.

II.—The maximum of passengers allowed, not more than 3 adults besides driver; in Family *tongas*, 3 adults and 2 children may be admitted.

III.—The maximum weight allowed for luggage per *Tonga* is one and half maund, Family *tonga* one maund only.

IV.—Every *Tonga* to be drawn by two ponies not over 13·2 in height, quiet, and well-broken in, and one pony from Murree to Tret and one pony from Murree to Kohala.

V.—A *tonga* is not allowed to carry more than 3 passengers besides the driver, and one and half maunds luggage; Family *tongas*, 3 adults 2nd 2 children and one maund luggage.

H. H. G. ROTTON,
District Superintendent of Police.

NOTICE.—Passengers disregarding the rules are liable to be prose cuted by the Police.

RULES, KASHMIR SECTION.

I.—*Tongas* will not run on the Kashmir road after dark.

II.—No return tickets are issued between Srinagar and Murree and *vice versâ*.

III.—Tolls, *ghâ-charai* and all other taxes are payable by the travellers.

IV.—Travellers will be conveyed strictly in the order of booking, and not more than six special *tongas* between Rawalpindi and Murree and four between Srinagar and Murree each way will be available daily. Half fare must be paid in advance, which will be forfeited if the *tonga* is not availed of on the day and time fixed for starting at the time of booking.

V. No *tonga* or bullock train cart can be supplied from any intermediate station between Rawalpindi, Murree, Baramulla and Srina-gar, or for a shorter distance than between these stations. But if seats are available in the Mail *tonga*, travellers may be taken at two rupees eight annas (Rs. 2-8-0) a seat per march.

VI.—Travellers are requested not to detain the *tonga* carrying Her Majesty's Mail for any reason whatever.

VII.—No seat or *tonga* to be considered secured till full fare has been paid and receipt obtained from the Agency. Intending travellers are requested to enter themselves the booking of their seats or *tongas* in the Diaries kept in the Agencies.

ote —As only four special *tongas* per day can be booked between Srinagar and Murree and *vice versâ*, more cannot be booked unless the travellers accept the risk of disappoint-ment and consequent delay for not being passed through on the day of their arrival. The observance of this rule is absolutely necessary to ensure the good working of the horses

the journey on payment of the prescribed
fee, as mentioned below, and by previous
arrangement with the Booking Agent at
office of starting.

For each day or part of day during which the
journey is broken Rs. 10; if broken without such previous arrangement it will be
held to terminate the journey.

Note.—A halt of not more than two hours for the purpose of re-
freshment or of two nights at any staging bungalow
between Murree and Baramulla only will not be considered
as a break of journey.

IX.—All luggage to be considered as under the traveller's charge and carried at his own risk.

The time of journey is as follows :—

	Hours.
Between Rawalpindi and Murree	6
,, Murree and Baramulla, inclu-sive of two nights' halt as permitted by rule	48
,, Baramulla and Srinagar ...	6

X.—The weight of luggage per seat allowed free
is 12 seers by the Mail *tonga*, luggage
exceeding 12 seers, but not exceeding one
maund, and then only if there is room in
the *tonga*, will be charged for separately
at the rates specified in the schedule for
articles carried by *tonga*.

Note.—The Agents have strict orders to weigh all luggage and to
charge for all in excess.

Travellers will be liable to forfeiture of fare, if insisting
upon any infraction of this rule, as the Agents have
instructions not to start *tongas*, but under this rule.

XI.—The Imperial Carrying Company give public notice that they will not be responsible for any injury, or the result of any injury, to the persons of passengers travelling by their service between Rawalpindi and Srinagar, or to loss or damage of their property, conveyed thereby, from any cause whatever.

XII.—Heavy packages for Kashmir must be sent at least ten days in advance to ensure their reaching destination before arrival of travellers.

XIII.—All goods and parcels are carried by the Company at owner's risk.

A. C. TALBOT, LT.-COL.,
Resident in Kashmir.

SPECIAL NOTICES.

(See Rule 28 under " General Rules ").

NOTICE.

The attention of the public is hereby invited to the provisions of the Stamp Law of the State, which require the receiver of a sum exceeding twenty rupees to give a stamped receipt when such receipt is demanded from him by the payer, the receiver being punishable with a fine of one hundred rupees if he declines to give the receipt. The receipt stamps of the Kashmir State will be used for the purpose, which dealers can procure at post offices in the districts as well as at the Srinagar Post Office.

Purchasers of articles and goods are accordingly advised, in their own interest, to obtain a stamped receipt when they pay money to dealers in Kashmir.

BHAG RAM,
Revenue Member of Council.

TOLLS ON THE JHELUM VALLEY ROAD.

1. Notice is hereby given that the Kashmir State levies the following taxes on the Jhelum valley road, the collection of which is leased to a Contractor.

I.—Road Tax (*Sarkana*) as follows :—

	Rs.	A.	P.
On each two-wheeled Carriage or *Tonga*	1	0	0
,, ,, *Ekka*	0	4	
,, ,, Cart drawn by 4 bullocks, laden	0	12	0
,, ,, ,, ,, unloaded	0	6	0
,, ,, 2 bullocks, laden	0	4	0
,, ,, ,, unloaded	0	2	0
,, ,, Camel, laden	0	8	0
,, ,, ,, unloaded	0	4	0
,, ,, Horse, laden ...	0	1	6
,, ,, ,, unloaded		0	9
,, ,, Ass, laden		0	6
,, ,, ,, unloaded ...		0	3
,, ,, Palanquin drawn by 8 *Kahars* (Bearers)	1	0	0
,, ,, ,, ,, 6 ,,	0	12	0
,, ,, ,, ,, 4 ,,	0	8	0
,, ,, ,, ,, 2 ,,	0	4	0
,, ,, Goat, Sheep and Pig		1	0
,, ,, Foot person ...		0	3
,, ,, Mule, laden ...		1	6
,, ,, ,, unloaded ...		0	9
,, ,, Cart drawn by 3 bullocks, laden	0	9	0
,, ,, ,, ,, ,, unloaded	0	4	6
,, ,, Bullock, laden ...	0	1	0
,, ,, ,, unloaded		0	6
,, ,, *Karrachi* (Roofed cart), laden, drawn by 2 bullocks	0	6	0
,, ,, *Karrachi* (Roofed cart), unloaded, drawn by 2 bullocks	0	3	0

II.—Grazing Tax (or *Gha-charai*) at 6 pies for each animal per stage.

2. As there are 8 stages from Kohala to Baramulla, it follows that animals going right through to or from Baramulla, must pay 4 annas each. Thus for through travellers the tolls payable on a *tonga* aggregate Rs. 1-8-0 *i.e.* Re. 1° road tax and 8 annas razing tax:

on an *ekka* the tolls aggregate 8 annas; on riding horses and ponies marching in unladen 4 annas 9 pies, on the same when laden 5 annas 6 pies each, and so on.

3.   To avoid inconvenience to travellers and visitors, arrangements have been made to collect both the road tax and the grazing tax either at Kohala or Baramulla.

Travellers and visitors are therefore requested to make payments, on account of these taxes, to the Contractor's Agent at the places above mentioned.

The Contractor's Agent will give receipts for the payments made to him.

4.   Ordinarily, travellers proceeding to Srinagar from British India should pay these tolls to the Contractor's Agent at Kohala and those returning to British India should pay at Baramulla.

5.   These tolls are exclusive of the ferry tolls paid at the Kohala bridge to the British Government.

6.   Travellers are responsible for payment of the taxes and not the proprietors of the *tongas*.

KASHMIR RESIDENCY: (Sd.) H. S. BARNES,
SRINAGAR, 15*th May*, 1895.   *Resident in Kashmir.*

NOTICE.

Notice is hereby given that on and after 1st November, on application to the Governor of Kashmir, visitors and residents in Kashmir will be supplied with firewood from a depôt, which is being formed near the Lal Mundi palace, at the following rates :—

Hutbas, 2 kharwars per rupee.
Zanglu, 2 kharwars, 4 traks per rupee.
Pinewood, 3 kharwars per rupee.

2. Application must, in all cases, be made, not at the depôt, but to the Governor, who will endorse on the application an order for the wood required. The application so endorsed will be taken by applicant's servant to the Munshi at the depôt, who will see that the wood is promptly supplied.

3. In all cases cash payment at the rates above given must be made at the depôt before delivery of the wood is given.

4. Wood will only be delivered to purchasers at the depôt. Applicants for firewood must make their own arrangements for taking to their homes the wood purchased. The Governor will always, if necessary, be ready to assist applicants to obtain boats for this purpose.

5. In order that there may be an ample supply of wood for all, no more than 500 *kharwars* of wood can be sold to one and the same family. Visitors and residents who require more than this amount, must purchase in the open market.

KASHMIR RESIDENCY,
    SRINAGAR :   }   H. S. BARNES,
The 25th September, 1895. }   *Resident in Kashmir.*

NOTICE.

European visitors and residents in Kashmir are informed that from and after 1st *Baisakh*, 1953 (12th April, 1896), under the orders of the Kashmir State Council, an annual tax will be levied on all boats owned and

employed in the valley of Kashmir, according to the
following schedule :—

	Rs.	A.	P.
House boat, 1st class	7	0	0
Do. 2nd class	5	c	
Do. 3rd class	4	c	
Doonga or large Kashmiri living boat, 1st class	3	0	0
Do. do. 2nd class ...	2	0	0
Do. do. 3rd class	1	4	0
Do. do. 4th class ...	1	0	0
Shikara or small Kashmiri boat, per *shikara* ...	0	8	0
Boats used for shali, *bhoosa* and wood, 1st class ...	2	0	0
Do. do. 2nd class ...	1	0	0
Khachu boats used for stones, lime, earth, &c. ...	1	0	0

2. The boats will be classified under arrangements
to be made by the Governor of Kashmir, who will keep
a list of all boats liable to the tax

3. The tax will be payable by the owner and not by
the occupier of a boat, and payment should be made
on demand in British Government rupees or their
equivalent in Kashmir coin.

KASHMIR RESIDENCY,
    SIALKOT :
16th November, 1895.

H. S. BARNES,
Resident in Kashmir.

———

NOTICE.

The Kashmir Darbar having introduced a Civil Transport Corps to assist in the requirements of travellers
between Srinagar and Gulmarg and Gulmarg and
Baramulla, the following rules (sanctioned by the
Kashmir State Council under Resolution No. 9, dated

Kashmir) regulating the employment of this transport,
are published for information of the public :—

1.   The Transport Corps will only work from the
15th April to the 15th October of each year.

2.   Transport can only be obtained at Srinagar,
Gulmarg and Baramulla.

3.   Requisition for transport at Srinagar should be
addressed to Rai Sahib Amar Nath, but at Gulmarg and
Baramulla to the Transport Agent.

4.   Requisitions for transport must be delivered to
the Rai Sahib or the Transport Agents, as the case
may be, at least 30 hours before the transport is
required.

5.   Applications for transport will be booked according to priority of receipt. In the event of all the
coolies and ponies at a stage being already engaged
for the day, any further requisitions for transport on
that day will be returned with an intimation to that
effect.

6.   Persons must avail themselves of the transport
for which they have indented on the day and at the
time mentioned in their requisitions, otherwise their
requisitions will be considered cancelled, and they will
be liable to pay half rates for the transport entered in
their requisitions.

7.   A voucher in duplicate will invariably be fur
nished when the transport is supplied   Travellers are
requested to sign one voucher as an acknowledgment of
the receipt of transport entered therein and return it to
the Transport Officer by whom it is presented: the
duplicate copy should be kept in case of any cause for
complaint arising.

8.   The rates for hire of transport under these rules
are :—

	Rs.	A.	P.
For each coolie ...	0	4	0
,. ,, *kahar*	0	7	0
,, a baggage pony ...	0	12	0
,, ,, riding pony with English saddle	1	0	0

These rates are for each full stage or distance less
than a full stage.

9.   Each coolie will carry a load of 25 sérs and each
pony one of two maunds.

These are the maximum weights, and must not be
exceeded.

10.   On arrival at their destination (or at Magam,
in the case of a journey between Gulmarg and Srinagar),
travellers are requested to dismiss the transport engaged
by them with the least practicable delay.

11.   The journeys between Srinagar and Gulmarg,
and Baramulla to Gulmarg, and *vice versâ,* as also from
Gulmarg to Palhalan (in cases when the transport is
taken from Gulmarg to that place) will be charged as
two full stages. In the case of the former journey,
transport must be changed at Magam, in the cases of
the two latter journeys, coolies will not be changed on
the road.

12.   In cases when a halt is made during any
journey, half rates only will be charged in respect of
each day that such halt may last.

13.   In all cases baggage will only be carried at
the owner's risk.   All possible precaution will, however,
be taken to guard against damage and loss, and assistance will be given in investigating circumstances under
which damage or loss may have occurred.

14. All complaints against the transport staff should be made to Rai Sahib Amar Nath at Srinagar.

15. Employers of transport are, in no case, to take the law into their own hands by attempting to deal with causes of complaint themselves; contravention of this rule will be brought to the notice of the Resident in Kashmir.

16. Visitors are reminded that, under the published rules, payment for coolie and pony transport must be made in advance to the Transport Agent and not to the coolies or pony men. If payment is not made in advance, the Transport Agent has authority to refuse to supply transport.

17. It is requested that the Transport Agent be treated with the consideration due to officials of His Highness the Maharajah of Jammu and Kashmir.

AMAR SINGH, RAJAH,

VICE-PRESIDENT,

Jammu and Kashmir State Council.

Approved—

A. C. TALBOT,

Offg. Resident in Kashmir.

GILGIT ROAD.

RULES FOR REST-HOUSES.

Tragbal.	Godhay.
Garai.	Astore.
Gurais.	Dashkin.
Pushwari.	Doian.
Burzal Chowki	Bunji.
Chilim Chowki.	Big Stone.

1. The rest-houses are provided, in the first place, for the use of European and Kashmir officials whose duties oblige them to travel on the road: European travellers are also allowed to occupy them on the understanding that officials have the first claim to the accommodation.

2. No servants, followers, or ponies are, on any account, to occupy the rest-houses.

3. Out-houses are erected for servants and followers, and where *serais* exist, they are available for the use of coolies, ponies, &c.

4. The *chowkidar* will supply, on payment, wood for the use of officials, travellers and their private servants, also grass for private ponies. It must be distinctly understood that he is not to be called on to supply wood for coolies, &c., nor grass for hired ponies.

5. A fee of annas eight per day is to be paid to the *chowkidar* by each person using the rest-houses only.

The Engineers directly in charge of the road are exempt from this rule.

6. A book is provided at each rest-house, in which all persons are requested to enter their names, date of arrival and departure, and the fee paid by them in accordance with rule. Payment under rule 5 must invariably be made. If any cause of complaint arise, it can be referred to the State Engineer, Jammu and Kashmir State.

AMAR SINGH,
Vice-President of State Council.

Approved—

A. C. TALBOT,
Resident in Kashmir.

FINIS.

W. Newman & Co.'s — — Indian Publications.

THE INDIAN AMATEUR SERIES.

Indian Amateur Gardener.—By "LANDOLICUS."
Practical Hints on the Cultivation of Garden Flowers and imported Vegetable Seeds, adapted for the plains of Bengal, the N.W. Provinces and Hill Stations, from notes compiled during eighteen year's experience of gardening in India. Illustrated. Crown 8vo, cloth. Rs. 6.

Indian Amateur Rose Gardener.—By "LANDOLICUS."
Practical Directions for the Cultivation and Propagation of Roses in the plains and Hill Stations of India. Second Edition. With four plates and 29 Woodcuts. Crown 8vo., cloth. Rs. 3.

Indian Amateur Dairy Farm.—By "LANDOLICUS."
Containing most useful information for the Dairy Farmer on Dairy Cattle Management, Milk, Cream, Butter, Cheese, the Production of Meat, Goats Goat, milk, Pigs, Poultry, Rabbits, Pigeons, with a chapter on Bees, and their treatment in India. With 31 Wood-cut Illustrations. Crown 8vo., cloth. Rs. 5.

Indian Amateur Poultry Book.—By "LANDOLICUS."
Containing clear and concise instruction for the successful management of Poultry in India, for both pleasure and profit. Illustrated by 22 Woodcut Illustrations in the text and 13 full-page Plates. Crown 8vo., cloth. Rs. 3

W. Newman & Co.'s — — Indian Publications.

Dainty Dishes for Indian Tables.—Fifth Edition, revised up to date. Crown 8vo., cloth, 447 pages.   Rs. 6

Veterinary Aide-Memoire and Receipt Book.—For the use of Non-professional Horse-owners in India. By Brigr.- Genl. W. H. RYVES. 8vo., cloth.   Rs. 6

The North Punjab Fishing Club Anglers' Hand book.—Compiled by G. H LACY (Bengal) Staff Corps, and thoroughly revised and corrected up to date, with several new chapters and additional information by Surgeon-Major E. CRETIN, Bengal Medical Service. Third Edition.   Rs 8.

Newman's Handbook to Calcutta.—Historical and Descriptive, with a plan of the City. Third Edition, revised and enlarged. Crown 8vo., cloth.   Rs. 4.

Newman's Handy Household Calculator.—Containing Tables of Interest, Wages and other useful informat on for the Household.   Re.

Manual of the Treatment of Children in India.—From birth up to 15 years of age. By Dr. S. C. AMESBURY M. R. C. S , L. R. C. P. Second Edition.   Rs. 3-8.

Hindustani Manual; or, The Stranger's Indian Interpreter. Consisting of a Concise Grammar, easy useful sentenees and a vocabulary of about 5,000 words. By J. F. BANESS, F. R. G. S., F.S. Sc. Pocket size, cloth.   Rs 2.

Household Hindustani.—A Manual for New comers, especially adapted for Ladies' use. By M. C. REYNOLDS Fifth Edition, revised.   As. 12.

CPSIA information can be obtained
at www.ICGtesting.com
Printed in the USA
BVOW11s1009120318
510355BV00031B/1315/P